From the Library of:

_____

The List

The List

BY
RICH KOSLOWSKI

3 Finger Prints

3 Finger Prints
3962 N. Prospect Ave., Shorewood, WI 53211

This 3 Finger Prints book is a premium edition July 2007 First Printing

10 9 8 7 6 5 4 3 2 1

Front cover design by C.J. Bettin

Book production by Max Estes

Edited by Rob Venditti and Wayne Beamer

Manufactured in the United States of America

Printed at Mas Graphics, Menomonee Falls, WI MasGraphics.com

For information regarding orders, bulk discounts, or signings and promotional events contact us at RichK@RichKoslowski.com

ISBN-13: 978-0-9794801-0-2
ISBN-10: 0-9794801-0-8

Graphic Novels—Fiction
Illustrated Novels—Fiction
Christmas—Fiction
Action/Adventure—Fiction
Science Fiction

ALSO BY RICH KOSLOWSKI

Graphic Novels

The King
Three Fingers

Comic Book Series

The 3 Geeks
Geeksville

Previous works and original artwork available at:
RichKoslowski.com

This one's for that little kid still inside the cynical grown-up...Longing for the Christmas magic of our youth.

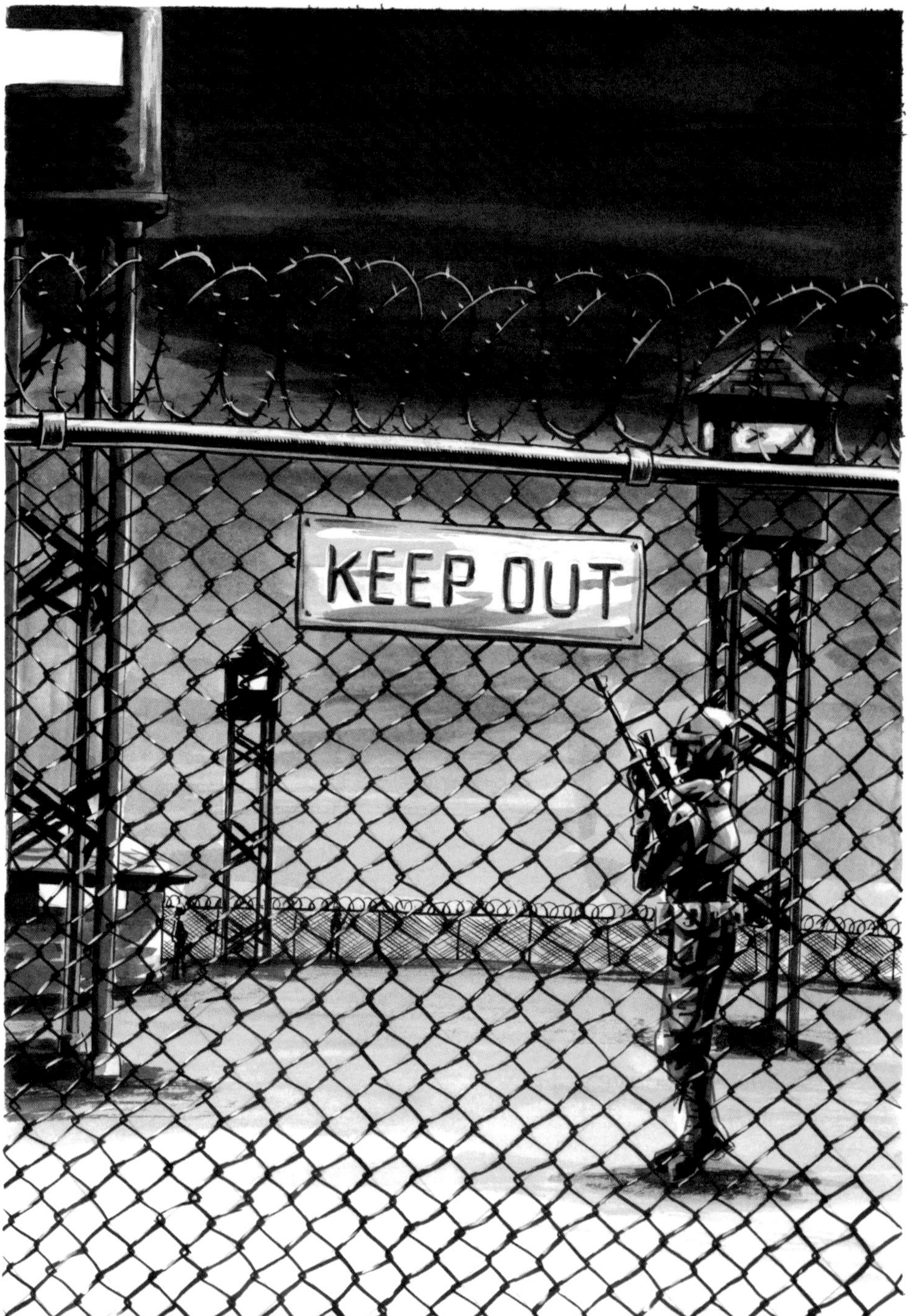
KEEP OUT

PROLOGUE:

The ones in the guard towers had heaters. Not so with the patrols on the ground. They walked the perimeter at a brisk pace, not only because it was their duty, but also to stay warm: nighttime in the desert is cold. They felt the intense heat from the blast almost before they heard the deafening sound. From above—from out of the darkness they came—without a warning…dozens of them! All the defense perimeters and technologies were caught completely unawares. The battle that followed was brief. Brutal but brief, with the attackers emerging victorious and with few casualties.

The attackers quickly sectioned off into two units: Unit One with the task of removing the bodies of the fallen guards, Unit Two with setting up an inner perimeter within the compound's outer perimeter—this one much smaller and with a completely different objective. They set up around an unmarked, nondescript area of the desert floor. Equipment and tools of all kinds were unpacked. They began drilling a large hole into the ground, twelve inches in diameter and four feet in depth. They arm the hole with explosives and stand back to detonate. The explosion is tremendous—The crater it leaves large enough to fit a city bus. Several move in quickly with shovels and remove more dirt until they find what they're looking for—a large metal loop. One of them signals skyward. A long length of metal cable silently descends from the blackness above. Attached to the end of it is an enormous metal hook. They attach the large hook and cable to the loop and, once again, signal skyward. The thick cable pulls taut and the ground surrounding the crater tremors—the crater's edge erupting violently upward before crumbling. Slowly, a massive concrete block struggles up from the crater. It is a perfect cube, 10' x 10' x 10' in dimension, and weighing several tons. They set the block down near the hole it originated from and drill several smaller holes into it so that, once again, they can insert their explosive devices. They scramble back a safe distance and detonate this second series of charges.

The smoke and debris slowly clears and the attackers converge around the epicenter ringed with dust and rubble. Unit One has rejoined Unit Two as they have finished disposing of the guards. In the middle of the now-clearing dust and debris a figure is seen lying on the desert floor—a human figure, naked and shriveled.

One of the attackers approaches the figure lying there. Another asks, "Is he alive?" as the first checks the figure's vital signs. The first responds, "Yes…he lives." And they disappear up into the black night sky with that frail form just as they approached—without a sound, as if they were never there at all.

NOW...
SIX MONTHS LATER...

"How do you feel?"

"How long?"

The first hesitates before answering the question to his question. "Thirty-eight years," he says finally.

"Thirty-eight years." It comes out little more than a whisper.

They are all gathered in this large room, ornate in its woodwork and decor, saying little more. The one now talking to him wears the suit of the ones he does not trust. Others are clad in the traditional garbs of their respective clans. Some carry weapons and dress as if ready for war. But they all stand the same...Silent...Waiting. Waiting for the figure sitting in shadow to say more. He says nothing. Just sits there in the large chair, behind a behemoth of an oak desk, in silence. The first (the one who asked how he feels) approaches. He begins to introduce himself, but the seated figure interrupts, "Randy McMahon...Yes, I know who you are."

The man is taken by surprise, but manages a reply. "It's Randall, now."

The shadowed figure says, "You were always such a good boy. But you're not a good boy anymore…are you, Randy?"

"No, sir…I'm not," he says, looking down at his three hundred dollar wingtips. "I suppose I haven't been for quite a long time." He continues, looking back up now—back at the shadowed figure sitting before him, "I'd like to change that. I'm here to help."

THEN...
39 YEARS EARLIER...

They always came. Every few years they would come and ask him. And every time they would get the same answer. But still they came—never giving up—for centuries. Always thinking—hoping—it would be them that would convince him. But they never did. Always he said "No," and forever would he say the same. He told them that. Every time. And yet here they were again. Asking him yet again. This time they said it was different; there was a war. There were always wars…They always came during them. *The Vietnam War* was what they were calling this one. But he had heard this before…many times, in fact. He remained unimpressed.

And always they wore their suits.

"As I have said before a thousand times, and will continue to say a thousand times a thousand more, the answer is no."

The leader of this group of suits asked again—pleaded really, "But, sir, please understand what we are asking you! With this information we could prove to the world that our cause—this war —is *just!* We could instantly prove that the enemy is, in fact, a 'bad' person. That we are just in our fight to stop him! The support we would get from the people of the world would end this war immediately."

"Yes. It would end this war," he answered. "That it would. Of that I have little doubt. It is the wars that it would, undoubtedly, create afterwards that concern me. This knowledge…this power in the wrong hands would prove disastrous. If I divulge this information to one person I will be asked to do so for others. Where would it stop? It is a precedent that I will not set. I cannot."

The suits don't give up. They rarely do. And the discussion— the pleas—continues for some time, their voices echoing in the vast halls. This great castle has heard these pleas many times, always the same. The voices may be different, the languages as well, but the pleas are always the same. Always the same… only echoes.

Ultimately, the suits give up, leaving the warm interiors of the mighty castle for the bitter winter winds that howled without. The castle halls quiet once again. The man that refused them sitting stoic in his throne—his trusted aides beside him— vigilant in their silence.

"Always they come…Always with the same story...The same request," he sighs. "They do not understand that they would not be able to handle the temptation. Whether their motives be true today, or not, the power of this List would ultimately turn them." He holds The List in his hands. "This List is meant for one thing only, and ever it shall remain. The children are pure…Its magicks shall ever remain pure so long as its power is used for the good of the children."

This man—this imposing figure clad in dark red and white—

rises slowly from whence he sat. He walks away deep with thoughts. Dark thoughts that match the dark corridor he now pauses in. He turns back to his aides—his most trusted confidantes—his loyal and noble Elves.

"Begin the fortifications on the castle," says the man in red and white. "I fear darker days lie ahead."

And so it began…the war between man and Santa Claus.

***

The suits answered to other suits. Suits wearing better suits. The better suits weren't happy with the news but weren't really surprised. No, his refusal to turn over "The List" was expected. Expected and planned for. Planned for for decades, in fact. This latest war was just a convenient excuse for them to ask in a civilized manner: An attempt to avoid bloodshed, and a great deal of money. Waging war was an expensive proposition. And money was what this was all about after all. Sure, if he were to have handed The List over they would have done what they said and used it to end the war, but that was just another means to an end for them. What it really all boiled down to was money—just like it does with most wars. And why shouldn't they be the ones to profit from the end of the war? Someone was going to, weren't they? Someone always does.

So he wouldn't turn it over willingly. A setback. True. And not a minor one. No, saying that would be understating the situation. This *was* a serious setback. But they had a backup plan. The exact name for the operation (because they always name these things) was "Operation Snowstorm." Yes, they were prepared and they were ready.

And now was the time.

NOW...

"How many are left?" he asked.

"What? You mean besides us? None...this is it."
Randall hesitated before finishing. "I'm sorry, but from what I understand, they were all wiped out in the initial assault. No survivors. They're all gone."

The shadowed figure replied softly, "No...not all of them."

23

THEN...
38 YEARS EARLIER...

Operation Snowstorm occurred as planned on Christmas Eve 1968 and was a complete success. Well, almost a complete success. Things like this—operations of this magnitude—are bound to have minor...*glitches*. But one hundred percent is not a realistic outcome one can honestly hope for when planning an operation of such scope. No, these men knew that was impossible. In fact, their diagnostics calculated an eighty-six percent chance of succeeding at best. So, when the operation was over and the percentage ran back at eighty-eight percent efficiency they were all very pleased. All involved received a tidy little year-end bonus as a result.

Yes, there were some unforeseen incidents they hadn't planned for, but there always are. And that *is* planned for...the "unexpected." It always factors in for at least ten percentage points one way or the other. It's all about the numbers. Math. Science.

It was the "science" that was the key. There was no way of figuring the "magick." That was beyond them. They tried for decades to no avail. They wasted an enormous amount of time, and billions of dollars, trying to figure it out. It was a Dr. Frederick Von Allsburgh, an expert in the field of Quantum Physics, who finally suggested they completely abandon that line of thinking altogether and put all their focus on the *science* of the problem. His contention was—and finally convinced them that—science and magick were all but one and the same. Separated not by vast degrees of difference, but running almost along the same parallels and separated by minor degrees at most. He argued that it was all but a matter of semantics, and that they, as educated men, could bridge the minor gap—or at least get close enough that it should not matter. Again, it was all within the acceptable amount of percentages. Numbers. That's what scientists know…numbers.

And so, after decades of futile research and billions of dollars wasted, the answer came to Dr. Frederick Von Allsburgh and his team of twelve scientists after just four months. The solution: how to capture the entity known as Santa Claus.

It had always been the "Time-Travel" aspect of the operation that stymied them. The placement of operatives was never the problem. They would place thousands of well-trained operatives around the planet on Christmas Eve at selected locations where their research showed "good" boys or girls lived. There the operatives would wait until they spotted Santa and capture him. Sedatives, nets and stun guns were to be used; the stun guns similar to the modern day "Tazer" gun (these guys were ahead of their time). No, this part of the operation was the simple part.

But, again, the problem was Santa's manipulation of time. For decades it was surmised that some form of time-travel had to be being used by Claus to successfully traverse the globe and deliver toys to millions of children in but one night. And they were right. Santa did have the ability, technology and magicks to travel through, or stop time, for all but himself and his magickal helpers: the elves and reindeer. It was his ability and his alone. Thus had it always been. But the scientists did not know this for sure, or for how long, or how it worked.

They just theorized.

The scientists were right; he manipulated time. They just didn't know how. Or how he could still deliver toys to millions of children even *with* Time at a standstill. After all, Santa would still have to physically traverse the globe to all the millions of homes; even with Time stopped this would take him *years* within the frozen timeline. Another part of the magickal aspect of this equation they'd never fully understand.

But they knew numbers. And what is time but numbers: The continuous succession of numbers. They were, over time, able to devise a small device—powered by, and tethered to, a larger nuclear battery—which would attach to an individual and form a small temporal bubble around them allowing them to "slide through" time while the world appeared to stand still around them. But "standing still" was a bit of an exaggeration. In truth the world around them merely slowed down. But it slowed down very much and to such a drastic degree that it all but stopped. This allowed the agents to move at an incredible speed. But again, the energy required for such a "standing still" of time and space was so demanding that the timing of the operation had to be all but flawless. They could only provide the sufficient amount of energy this required for short periods of time. Just under a minute was the best they could achieve.

The factoring in of Claus's ability to actually stop time around him, not just slow it down, was also a concern. For, in essence, he would be able to move slightly faster than the operatives. Thus it was decided to scale down the amount of homes the operatives would be placed at, and increase the number of operatives at each home. It was also decided that they would synchronize an exact time that all operatives worldwide would initiate the plan and hope for the best. Their theory was that Santa stopped time at exactly midnight on Christmas Eve. It just made sense to them that this would and could be the only plausible time for him to do it.

They didn't tell the operatives about all the previous test runs and what happened to the test subjects. Losses were to be expected after all. Science is, by nature, trial-and-error.

3,756 men died that night in the capturing of Santa Claus. About 600 survived, most with severe brain and bodily damage. But they did capture him.

It was the convergence of two separate entities manipulating time in such close proximity. That and the differences in, not only the two separate entities—Claus and the operatives—but the operatives themselves. There were four operatives at every location and each of them was off to a slight degree of one another. The scientists found it impossible to calibrate each operative's individual Time Suppressors exactly with each other's. So they were all off by the most infinitesimal of margins, but off nonetheless. The result of which proved catastrophic. It was the convergences of these five differently manipulated and altered timelines which was what actually ended up incapacitating Santa Claus, not any of the more conventional methods they had planned. He was knocked unconscious, and the four operatives were killed instantly; their bodies pulped beyond recognition. *Halcyon's* top scientists had planned for this possible outcome too, of course…They gave it a thirty-two percent chance of happening. The clean-up operation cost them millions…the cover-up millions more.

Phase two of Operation Snowstorm—the occupation of the North Pole— was synchronized with Phase one—the capture of Santa Claus. They were to attack simultaneously with the attempted capture whether it was successful, or not. It was an "all or nothing" plan.

The attack on Santa's castle was horrible.

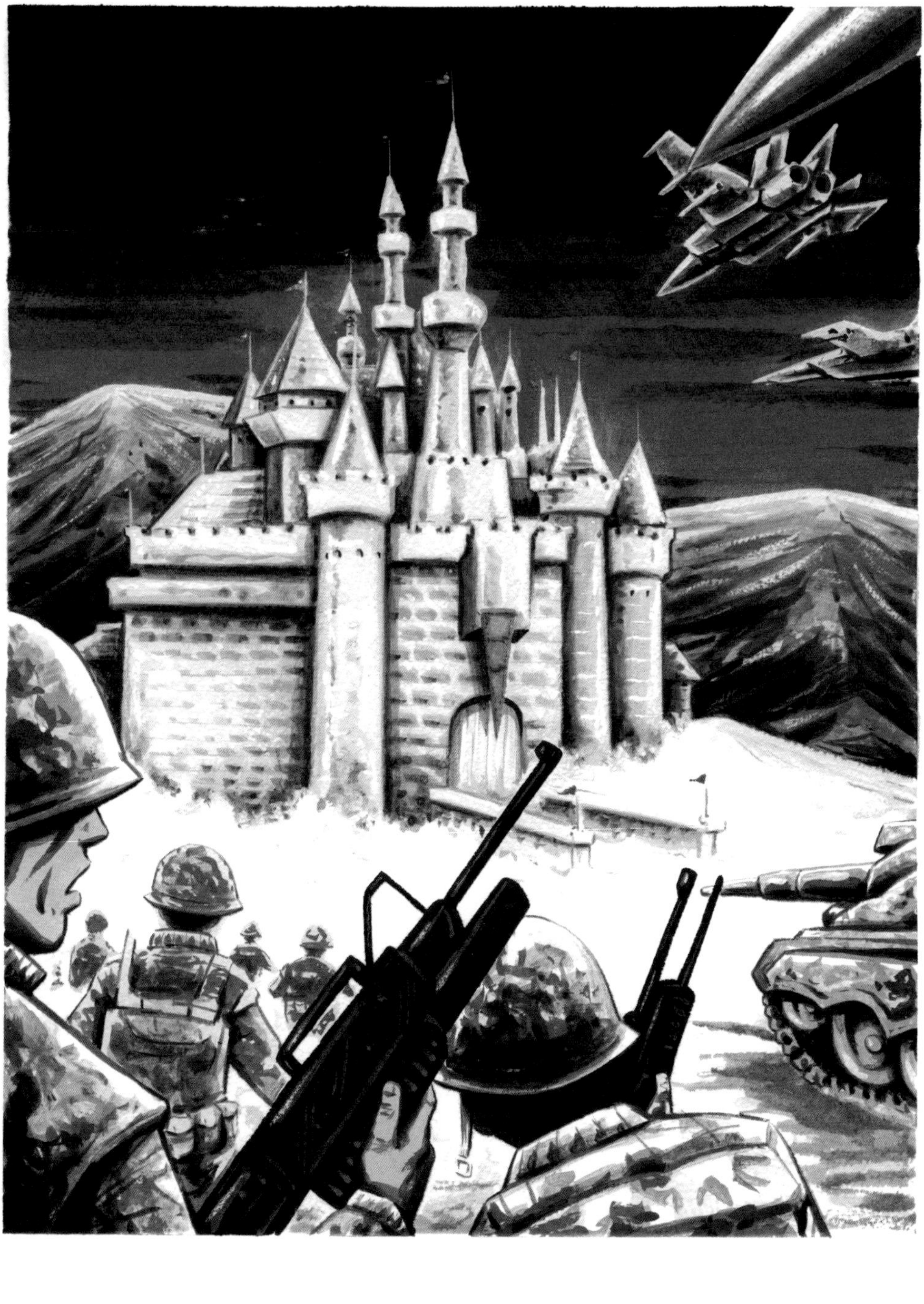

NOW...

"What do you mean *'not all of them'*?" asked Randall. "There are others?!"

"In due time," he replied. "But first I have some questions of my own."

Randall calmed himself. He was anxious about the comment made regarding "others." He needed to know what that meant, but respected this man's need to have his own questions answered first. And he suspected there would be many before his own would be addressed again.

Randall patiently replied, "Of course, sir. You must have many."

"Who are they?" was the first.

THEN...

They weren't the government of a powerful country as most that came before him were. They weren't even the government of a small country, looking to become a powerful country. They weren't a faction, or splinter group looking to form their own government. And they weren't the occasional fanatical religious group with the deranged idea of "saving the world." No, they were different than all the others that came before him. They were a business. A corporation. *The Halcyon Corporation, Inc.* Halcyon: in Greek mythology, a bird resembling the kingfisher, believed to have had the power to calm the waves at the time of the winter solstice when it nested at sea. They weren't in it to save the world; they were in it to turn a buck...a *whole lot* of bucks actually.

The Halcyon Corporation was founded towards the end of the nineteenth century by Sir Stephen T. Carlson—the son of an English nobleman. Halcyon had their fingers in many different pies: newspapers and telegraph communications, importing/

exporting and the distribution of packaged goods, and they also partially funded the development of certain advancements in technologies of the time like electrical conductors and such. Later, after the turn of the century, the field of communications and technologies became flooded with competitors and they shifted their interests towards the procurement of lands and developments of those lands.

Real estate.

They acquired substantial acreages throughout the upper region of the Midwestern United States and lower provinces of Canada. Although originally based in Europe and still maintaining a foothold there, European land was finite and expensive to obtain. The "New World" was vast and one could still purchase prodigious acreages at bargain rates. This was how Halcyon made its fortune. And its fortune was exceptional.

But not enough. No. Never enough.

By the mid-twentieth century, Sir Stephen T. Carlson was in his seventies and the corporation had grown to include additional shareholders. There were seven shareholders in all, including Sir Stephen, with Sir Stephen still holding the majority of stock. Halcyon was powerful with money but it only went so far. They could influence politics and government to a degree—manipulate the parties through "contributions"— but still it was not enough. There were limits to what they could achieve through these means.

Halcyon wanted more. The men of Halcyon wanted more. Why waste time and money on manipulating governments when one can be their own government? Halcyon was well versed in procurement, after all; it was how they made their fortune. In the business world they were a world power: What was the difference between the business world and the political world, really, anyways? And so, a vote was taken by the principal shareholders and it was unanimous…Halcyon would become their own country. The problem was that this would never happen on European or North American soil where they had the majority of their land and assets. No, the legalities were imposing and the thought of some sort of secession impossible. Besides, even though they had the monies to obtain the armies and weapons necessary, the thought of any sort of attack on North American soil was ridiculous.

The decision was easy, really. And it came to them rather quickly. Attack and conquer a sovereign state: well-positioned, well-armed, and in an economical situation that would immediately profit the corporation and establish them as a world power.

The North Pole…the land of Santa Claus.

Long known throughout the governments of the world to be a place of great power, not only on a magical, mythical level, but an economical one as well. True, Santa Claus worked the North Pole with no aspirations of profit or power, as his was an almost "Holy" place in this world. Revered by most, questioned by others, but still untouchable. Even if one wanted to attack this magical place, for some reason, it would be utter folly. His forces were formidable, the castle impregnable. Ask the few who tried in decades past. Theirs were lessons hard learned. Long ago did Santa realize he had what others might want and the reality was that he must protect it…whatever the cost. He was a peaceful man, an honorable man, a Holy man, but even the holiest of men must sometimes defend what is theirs. And defend it he had.

First there were the Elves. The kindest, gentlest, most noble of creatures. Pure of heart, loyal, and a harder working soul one never will find. And if angered, fierce beyond measure—their stature deceptive: masking a physical strength tempered by centuries of living in the harshest of conditions—their stamina as well. These noble creatures, if tested, made up an almost impenetrable, immovable ground force.

From the air they were protected by the reindeer. The flying reindeer. Magical creatures of flight and speed. And there were thousands of them. Led by the "Elite Eight" that guided Santa's sleigh. The most honored and almighty of them all... His generals.

And the weapons…forged by the Elves combining ancient magicks and unearthly technologies. Mighty weapons of energy. Protective armors and enchantments. Weapons beyond conventional descriptions or analysis. Beyond human comprehension and means to combat.

And there were other forces…rumors and whispers of things seen and unseen on the battlefield. Unthinkable things. If to be believed would be utter madness.

And leading them all was their King; the great one known by

many different names…Roman Befana, Pere Noel, Julenisse, Germanic Berchta, Christkindl, Sanct Herr Nicholaas, Sinter Klaas, Sankt Nikolaus, Kriss Kringle, Saint Nicholas, Father Christmas…*Santa Claus*. The most benevolent of all beings. An elemental force of nature. Neither man nor god but something akin to both. Altogether both, yet neither. Kind and generous beyond description. To give, his sole purpose in this life. A being of such honor and nobility and love. Pure goodness. Mighty and mythic.

How does one defeat an army whose King is akin to a god?

They kill the King.

NOW...

"Halcyon," he grumbled. "Yes...I remember them. They were one of the many of the men in suits who came before me. A company of...*questionable* standards."

"Not always," said Randall. "Not at first."

THEN...

The postcards were Peter's favorite part. His idea. Most all of this was his idea, actually. He'd been planning this for as long as he could remember, really. Yes, a very long time. Peter Valentine was his name now. One of the principal shareholders––one of the seven–– of The Halcyon Corporation and the "Right Hand Man" of Sir Stephen T. Carlson. Peter was the one who had Sir Stephen's ear. It was Peter. The other five shareholders sometimes called him the Puppet Master—which was ironic considering his height.

Peter joined Halcyon in 1955 when Sir Stephen, strapped for liquid cash, went public with stock in the company. Peter had been waiting. He'd had his eye on Halcyon for a long time. Decades. It was the "Wyoming Lower Twelve" deal that did it. Halcyon purchased twelve separate land deals in the southwest region of Wyoming. The twelve lots, although sold by several different parties, were all adjoined, and having them all would encompass over 100 million acres of beautiful open range. Halcyon's plan was to develop the outer portions of the land into high-end ranches, and build a small city at the center with housing, shops, businesses, etc. The plan was massive in scope and if successful would make Halcyon the largest, most profitable, privately owned company in the world.

The plan failed. A lawsuit was filed against Halcyon by a Native American group claiming ownership of the land. This was 1953, and in 1953 not much merit was given to claims such as these. The Native American had even less rights than the African American in the 1950s. And, normally, a claim like this was quickly swept under the rug. A payment made here and there, some bribes and threats and they would go away. But this time it was different. This time the Native American group— calling themselves "The Black Feathers"—was organized. Galvanized. And apparently had some "big money," and high-priced lawyers, behind them. They didn't back down.

The lawsuit was costing Halcyon millions to fight, and every day that the land lie there undeveloped cost Halcyon even more money. They couldn't develop it, they couldn't unload it; they were landlocked and it was killing the company financially. Sir Stephen had no choice but to look for investors.

Peter Valentine had been waiting. He was the first to come on. And Sir Stephen loved him. Peter was young, good-looking, energetic and full of ideas. He was also brash and arrogant: headstrong. Sir Stephen saw a lot of himself in young Peter and a bit of what he wished he had been. Other investors came on as well (the other five shareholders) and the company was made whole again. Eventually the lawsuit was settled, and it was business as usual at Halcyon. In the long run the company grew even stronger with the addition of shareholders. And Peter blazed a trail with fresh ideas and innovations.

Yes, there was no doubt that Sir Stephen loved him...Trusted him. It seemed as if Peter had almost cast a spell on Sir Stephen.

How could he even begin to suspect that Peter orchestrated the whole thing?

NOW...

"What do you mean it was *'the postcard'*?" asked the man in shadow.

Randall opened a large manila envelope he'd been holding and reached inside. He removed an old postcard from it. "This was the first. There were many after. They came every year."

The man in shadow read the postcard, his face turning red with anger. He turned it over several times, reading and rereading it. He handed it back to Randall.

"People believed...how could they not? It seemed plausible," said Randall.

"And you worked for these people?"

"I did, sir, yes. I-I do..." he said. "But that was before I knew the truth. It was a good job...a good opportunity. I thought I was doing the right thing."

"And when did you realize you weren't?"

"I'd suspected for a while...a few years...but..."

"But the money was good?"

"Yeah...the money was good. I made a lot of money." Randall looked ashamed.

THEN...
37 YEARS AGO...

"Dear Parents of all the good little boys and girls around the world!

Greetings from the North Pole! Christmas time is almost here once again, but Santa needs **your** help this year! Due to budgetary restraints and there being **soooo** many good boys and girls around the world to deliver toys to, we're asking you to limit your Christmas lists to four toys this year!

Thank you and Merry Christmas!"

Please note: Due to logistical problems as well, some delivery of toys shall be made via U.P.S.

"So, what do you think?"

The other six members of the board sat silently. Finally one of them said, "This is going to cost us *a fortune!* Millions!"

"Billions, actually," said Peter, "and billions more over the next three to four years." He continued, "But ten years from now we'll have made it all back and ten times as much as that! This is a long-term investment, gentlemen! It takes money to

49

make money, remember?

"Next year the postcard will read that they should, again, limit themselves to four choices, but could they please enclose a check for five dollars to help defray the enormous costs of shipping. An insignificant fee, really, for the happiness of the children. The year that follows we'll ask that they limit the choices to three but that the fee shall remain at five dollars.

"It's the shipping that's going to cost us the most. We have the castle and the means to produce the toys…it's the delivery that's the real cost. And that'll be explained as well.

"Listen," Peter continued, "people just want their kids to be happy…to shut the hell up and leave them alone for awhile while they hit the eggnog. They're not going to balk at five measly dollars! Five bucks for three or four nice toys, *delivered?!...*It's a bargain. And anyone with common sense could make that 'leap of faith' and realize that, *'Heck, I guess it would be tough to deliver all them toys by hisself in one night! Makes sense he'd need a little help.'*

"Eventually the postcards will get to the point, over time, where the parents will be presented with two choices…*our* choices! A truck or army men for the boys, or a doll or makeup kit for the girls. And the fee will be ten dollars." The others seated around the large boardroom desk all listened intently to Peter. They were beginning to see where he was going with all of this. Their demeanors changed.

"After a couple years of the 'bland,' limited choices we offer, the next phase of postcards will be seen by them as something of a relief!" Peter continued triumphantly. "By the tenth year we will present them with some truly remarkable 'Package Deals!' They will be presented with several choices, at several different package prices. We'll have the 'Silver, Gold and Platinum Packages' offered for both girls and boys! Each package will consist of a variety of toys, the better the package the better the toys. And, of course, the price will reflect the better choices. The Silver package will be the old choices and stay at ten bucks—Gotta have something for the poor folks to pick—but the Gold package will have some nicer toys and cost fifty bucks! The Platinum package'll be for the folks with the *real* money! Five hundred bucks and their little brats are treated to a smorgasbord of wonderful little toys, gadgets, trinkets… *whatever!* You just wait and see how many parents, when given the choice, go for that Platinum deal! They're creatures driven by guilt, parents, and they don't want to feel cheap when it comes to their kids."

"We're going to be rich, gentlemen." It was Sir Stephen who spoke now.

"We're already *rich*, Sir Stephen," answered Peter. "We're going to be *gods*!"

51

NOW...

"I found it in my parents' dresser when I was twelve. They'd saved them all, I guess. I only took the one, hoping that that way they wouldn't notice. It was the first, I guess. I remember it really bothering me." Randall continued, "I was only twelve but everything started making sense to me now. For years we were told that you had to be a 'good' boy or girl or you wouldn't get any Christmas presents, and it worked. Most kids were good. And the bad ones didn't get presents. Simple.

"But over the years I started noticing that the bad kids were getting gifts as well as the good. And sometimes *better* gifts. I remember it really pissed me off. Why be a good kid all the time if it doesn't matter? I guess other kids noticed as well. You started seeing more and more bad behavior exhibited."

"Yourself included?" he asked, still sitting in the large chair behind the desk.

"I guess so," said Randall. "Nothing too terrible, though, really. Just little things…mouthing off more, stealing candy and junk. And whattaya know, come Christmas time there they were, all wrapped up from Santa. Didn't matter a bit."

"You lost it, didn't you? The spirit of Christmas."

"I suppose I did."

"And in me?"

"Yes. I'm sorry."

"Don't be…I can't blame you," he said. "When did you start working for them?"

"I started working for Halcyon right after I graduated from college. Data processing. Entry-level job, decent pay, and quickly moved up the ladder…the 'fast track.' I worked in their New York offices for the first six or seven years until I was asked if I wanted to relocate—supervise their shipping and receiving. I didn't really, but the pay increase was phenomenal."

"The North Pole?"

"At first I thought they were joking!" said Randall. "They weren't. I had the whole thing laid out to me—well, their version, anyways. It was explained to me how Halcyon was approached by you decades ago and asked to 'carry on' in your absence…that you were dying. Halcyon was well-suited, you said, for carrying the mantle and continuing the tradition. They told me, and many others, that they did it for the good of the children...the good of the entire world. I even had to sign a 'letter of confidentiality.'

"I'll admit, it sounded good. A bit far-fetched, sure, but I told myself, 'Hey, I'll be doing something good here…something important.' And looking at my paycheck at the end of each week didn't hurt any either."

"How did they explain that?" he asked.

"Not too many asked. I didn't. I just figured we all deserved it…that *I* deserved it."

"I see."

"I know. Like I said, I'm here to help now. I'd like to put things right."

He paused for a bit, digesting all of this. It had only been six months since they pulled him from the desert floor. For the first three months he couldn't even feed himself, so weak he was. After that it took him weeks to regain his speech and motor skills. Weeks more to fully understand what had happened. Thirty-eight years they had him buried. Thirty-eight years they carried on making billions of dollars in his name. He was furious. Angered beyond belief.

Finally he spoke, "And no one could do a thing to stop them." It wasn't a question.

"No," said Randall. "They couldn't."

"Because of The List."

"Yes," answered Randall. "Halcyon had The List."

THEN...
37 YEARS AGO...

"They'll never let us get away with it." It was another shareholder who spoke. Todd Lange was his name. His family's fortune was made in aviation. "The other governments."

"What are they going to do to stop us?" spat Peter. "We have The List! Even if we didn't have our army, we have The List."

The List. Santa's List. The thing that so many had come to him asking him for for so many centuries. The thing he had refused to give away so many times. Every time.

The List. *'Who is naughty, and Who is nice.'* *'He Knows... He has a List!'* A magical book with every single person on the planet's name in it. Their name and one of two simple words beside it; either *'Good'* or *'Bad.'* A powerful tome of information.

Information is Knowledge. *Knowledge is power!*

Halcyon had what everyone else wanted, and wanted for the same reason...POWER!

And if anyone tried to usurp them—any country or government tried to stop them—all Halcyon would have to do is use that power to thwart them. Share with the people of the world the information within this powerful book. Show them The List. Show them exactly who is *Naughty* and who is *Nice*.

There wasn't a single government on the planet that wanted that information made public.

They would be powerless to stop Halcyon—powerless to stop their takeover of Christmas. They would do the only thing they could do. Look the other way. Cover it up. Comply. Politics.

"No," said Peter with a smile, "they'll leave us alone."

NOW...

"So they had taken over Christmas. And no one could stop them."

"Not with you out of the picture," said Randall.

"Yes," he said, pausing, looking around the room at Randall and the others. Finally he continued, "How did you find me?"

THEN...
38 YEARS AGO...

They buried him in the Nevada desert—a vast, barren expanse of land owned by Halcyon. They couldn't kill him. They tried. But it was as they suspected, Santa was an immortal...he wouldn't be killed. So, they buried him: deep in the desert floor encased in a block of concrete. They didn't know what else to do with him, really. The ocean floor was suggested by someone, outer space by another, but it was decided that they should know where he was at all times and have access to him in case they needed to retrieve him for some reason (besides, shooting him into outer space would be extremely expensive). They didn't know what that reason might be, but they thought it a sound decision nonetheless.

The burial site would be guarded at all times. Fenced in and monitored by an elite, highly trained unit of armed guards and the best detection devices money could buy. Most didn't even know what it was that they were guarding. They simply thought they were a communications station or some such thing. Very few knew what was at the site, and why.

Very few.

Sir Stephen, Peter Valentine, the other five shareholders and a small handful of subordinates in charge of the security of the body.

But people talk. Eventually someone talks.

NOW...

"I got a memo."
"A *memo?!*"
"Yes…an inner office memo."
"From who?"

8 MONTHS AGO...

He woke up that morning with horrible pain. Unbearable. David Falstein-Droese III–one of the seven shareholders of Halcyon, Inc. It was his tooth…one of his molars. He popped four aspirin and headed into the office. They were all stationed there now. Headquartered at the North Pole. And why wouldn't they be? They thought the harsh weather would deter them but it didn't. The technologies there were so advanced that the area directly surrounding the castle was manipulated to maintain a more tolerable environment. And there were chambers within that were tropical paradises. Many and varied to suit any needs. The castle was paradise.

All the amenities were at their disposal as well: sport, recreation, entertainment, fine dining and medical care. Full medical and dental to be specific.

So, it was to the office that David Falstein-Droese III rushed that morning…to see the dentist.

NOW...

"The dentist."

"You received a memo from a dentist?"

"Yes...*the dentist.*"

The shadowed figure that was the being known to the world as Santa Claus rose quickly to his feet. "My God!" was all that he could manage.

***

He worked the private sector for decades. Happy. It was when his own family started receiving the postcards that he returned. He knew something was wrong. But returning wasn't a simple matter. It would require a great deal of planning and patience.

He applied and got in at one of the smaller regional offices in Ohio at first. There he worked diligently for several years, biding his time. He put in for a transfer and was relocated to the Mid-western regional headquarters in Chicago. There he moved up the ranks to chief of staff, Dental, and remained there for ten more years. He eventually worked his way up to National Junior Chief Of Staff at the New York facility where he stayed for the next four years. He was a model employee. And it seemed completely natural when he applied, was accepted and eventually transferred to their 'Crown Jewel' facility, their headquarters at the North Pole. There he remained and worked, gaining the trust of the shareholders and their most valued employees.

It was there, finally, where he learned the truth. From David Falstein-Droese III. It's amazing what people will say under the gas.

Now he just had to find someone to help him. Someone he could trust.

He had all the employee's medical charts and histories. And he made a point to see each and every one of the thousands of them at some point. He could've delegated the simple cleanings and check-ups to the dental assistants—as was standard practice—but he wouldn't get to know them that way. And Halcyon just attributed this "hands on" attention as excellent work   performance.

It was in this way that he met Randall McMahon. Randall had excellent charts.

***

"No cavities."

"Excuse me?"

"I had no cavities. He liked me because of that…trusted me."

"He would," said Santa, shaking his head.

"He started asking me questions. Just small talk, really…little things. He was very good…never tipped his hand. I think it was just his way of feeling me out, but I picked up on it right away." Randall continued, "I was curious so I made another appointment after the first one. Nothing was wrong with me. I think he sensed it. A month later I got the memo. It was vague but I knew who it was from and what it meant. It read, 'He lives.' That's it. That's all it said. I went back to my apartment and dug out the postcard. I took a chance and slid it under his office door the next day. A day later he sent it back with a note that said, 'There are others.'"

"Where is he now?" asked Santa, "Where's Norbie?" Saying his name out loud brought back a wave of powerful emotions and he had to fight to keep back the tears. Norbie was alive! He couldn't believe it. They didn't get him—That irritating little non-conformist who didn't want to make toys for him. An elf that didn't like making toys…Absurd! But Norbie was different…wasn't he? Norbie wasn't entirely Elf. He had human blood running through his veins as well. Centuries earlier a descendant's dalliance in the human's world had tainted Norbie's family bloodline. And so, he was…different. He didn't want to make toys. He wanted to fix teeth. But elves don't need dentists. Their legendary "sturdiness" precluded them from many of the ailments a human's "less sturdy" frame might succumb to. And so he left…into the human's world. He wasn't there when the castle was first attacked.

"He's still there…inside. We didn't think it wise to blow his cover," answered Randall.

"Can we communicate with him?"

"It's…ah…sort of taken care of. Norbie's got it all worked out."

"Good…Very good." Santa circled the room surveying the handful of them that saved him while he digested all of this information. There were some two-dozen. He was not yet back to full-strength, still a fraction of his former self, and yet he still towered over them. All of them. Especially the Elves.

"Mr. McMahon, I think it's time we told you of the 'others.'"

THEN...

Halcyon had planned for almost all contingencies. They did all the necessary calculations and ran hundreds of simulations before executing "Operation Snowstorm." They were meticulous to a fault. And the "insight" that Peter Valentine brought to the table seemed almost precognitive in nature...At times scary (Dr. Von Allsburgh would never admit it, but it was Peter who suggested he focus his studies on the *science* of the Time-Travel problem). But Peter Valentine came on at Halcyon in the mid-fifties. And Halcyon first approached, and was subsequently rejected by Santa, at the time of the Vietnam War—in the late sixties. 1967 to be exact. It was after this visit that Santa became troubled and ordered fortifications on the castle. Perhaps displaying a precognitive ability of his own. It wasn't only fortifications to the castle that took place, however. Additional changes took place. Changes that Halcyon could have never predicted or planned for.

MERE DAYS AGO...

Norbie had examined all but one of the four thousand some employees who worked and lived on the grounds here at the North Pole—or Halcyon, as it was known to its populace. He had even checked Sir Stephen himself on several occasions, conducting several dental procedures along the way. He found the man to be polite and patient, not at all the tyrant he had at first envisioned. Norbie wondered if it was only because of Sir Stephen's advancing years or if there were other factors involved.

No, the only citizen of Halcyon yet to be examined by Norbie was one of its principal shareholders: its senior advisor to Sir Stephen and second-in-command, Mr. Peter Valentine. Norbie tried repeatedly to set up an appointment without any success. Mr. Valentine's personal secretary always informing him that Mr. Valentine was unavailable—too busy. Norbie (or Dr. Herman J. Lember, as was the alias he worked under) urgently persisted, having already examined everyone else and learning all that he could from them; all the vital and important information possible. The six other shareholders—especially David Falstein-Droese III—had provided him with the most information and the most valuable information, but there was a limit to how much even they knew. It was Peter Valentine Norbie had to see. He had gathered from his previous "examinations" that Peter was the one really "pulling the strings" around here and that if there was anything more to be learned that he would be the one who knew it. And what Norbie needed to know was where The List was being kept. His best guess was that only Peter Valentine knew. He tried getting this specific bit of information from all the others he examined while having them under the influences of his very own special blend of "laughing gas," but none of them yielded anything useful. It became more than apparent to him that the five shareholders under Sir Stephen and Peter Valentine were merely here because of the monies they invested so many years ago—they were pawns and would not factor much in the outcome that lie ahead.

It was the company handbook that actually forced the issue—ironically written for the most part by Peter Valentine himself. Norbie cited company policy regarding mandatory physicals, pointing out that Mr. Valentine had, according to company records, never undergone one.

His secretary called him back the following day to set up an appointment.

In three more days Norbie the Dentist would meet Peter Valentine for the first time.

Again.

NOW...

"He told me there were 'others.' He never explained exactly what that meant," said Randall. "And when I pressed the issue he clammed up."

"He didn't know yet if he could completely trust you," said Santa.

"No, I guess not. Can't blame him. I did work for the enemy."

"He told you he was an Elf?"

"Yes."

"And that there were others, obviously?"

"Yes," said Randall while looking around the room at the Elves standing there with them.

"Did you ask him where they came from?" asked Santa.

"Of course! I was stunned to hear that any were left. Halcyon had told us that all were *'lost'* since your death, er...y'know... your *alleged* death."

"And what did he tell you?"

"He said that he 'found' them."

Santa actually chuckled very softly at this. "Norbie always

had a way of understating things."

"Wait a minute," said Randall, excited, "Are you telling me there are *more?*"

***

One of the contingencies that Halcyon failed to anticipate or plan for was the population explosion of the twentieth century. The worldwide population more than doubled from the end of the nineteenth century to the end of the twentieth. This rise in population didn't go unnoticed by Santa and his advisors. In fact it was something that they had always closely monitored and made adjustments for—one of the many tasks performed by the Elves through the centuries. By the 1950s Santa and his trusted Elves had already begun working on a plan to station "hubs" around the globe. Secret, hidden distribution sites where toys would be warehoused and Santa could pick them up as he traversed the globe on Christmas Eve night. Even with the ability to manipulate the time-stream Santa could only carry so many toys per trip. It made sense to have distribution sites scattered across the globe.

It was Santa's meeting with The Halcyon Corporation representatives in 1967 that caused them to expedite the installation of the hubs: that and the fortifications of the North Pole. Santa sensed "darker days" to come back in 1967, but, just like Halcyon, didn't anticipate the full scope of the darkness that lie ahead.

So the hubs were set up. There were hundreds of them. And at each site there would need to be Elves. Many, many Elves.

The Halcyon scientists were all about the numbers. And had they foreseen the installation of the hubs they would have easily calculated the number of Elves now scattered across the planet thirty-eight years later. There were hundreds of hubs, worked by dozens of Elves at each hub. Factor in the fact that Elves are very long-lived—just shy of being immortals themselves—and reproduce just like humans?

There were a lot of Elves. And they were waiting. Waiting for their King's return…waiting for the final battle. Waiting and making more Elves.

The increased worldwide population would factor against Halcyon again, in an entirely different way, before the final battle's outcome was determined.

***

"Th-There must be *thousands...tens* of thousands of them!" cried Randall. "What are we waiting for then? We should attack them now!"

"They have the castle, though," he answered back. "Even with tens of thousands of them we would be slaughtered."

"But they'd have *you* again! Leading them! That must count for something?!"

"Yes. But I am not yet fully recovered. And still they have The List," said Santa.

"I don't understand," replied Randall. "How does that affect the outcome? It's just a list...*a book.* I know it has powers but—"

"They know I have escaped. They've known for six months. Don't you think that they've anticipated some sort of an attack from us? They have, undoubtedly, used The List to fortify their armies."

"But-But they don't know about the Elves!...Maybe—"

Santa interrupted before Randall could finish. "Ease up, friend. All is not lost yet. We have other friends besides the Elves. Remember?"

Randall's eyes lit up. How could he be so stupid? He was there after all…there when they rescued him. Was it because they weren't human, or weren't Elves that he didn't consider them? "The Reindeer!" he shouted.

***

All but a handful of them were slaughtered when the armies of Halcyon attacked the castle. The few that escaped were scattered across the globe…hiding for years. The great thing about being a magical, flying reindeer was that they looked just like any other normal reindeer, so "blending in"—or "hiding in plain sight"—wasn't a big problem. Halcyon would have had to eliminate all the reindeer across the planet to ensure that they got them all.

Santa's Generals—his "Elite Eight" that led the sleigh—his most noble, most mighty—were all killed the night Santa was captured. But the few who escaped eventually found each other again. And just like the Elves they waited for Santa's eventual return. Just like the Elves they knew he was still alive. They were all linked together in some mystical way. The "magicks" of the Santa Claus were such. If he were to die they would have known. They would have known because they would have died as well. Such was the extent of their link.

So the few remaining reindeer waited. And just like the Elves, they made more reindeer while they did so.

***

When Norbie saw Peter Valentine sitting in his waiting room he froze. Suddenly he had answers to many of the questions that haunted him for the past few decades. He understood now how Halcyon managed to pull off the near impossible.

The big question now for Norbie was what was he going to do about it?

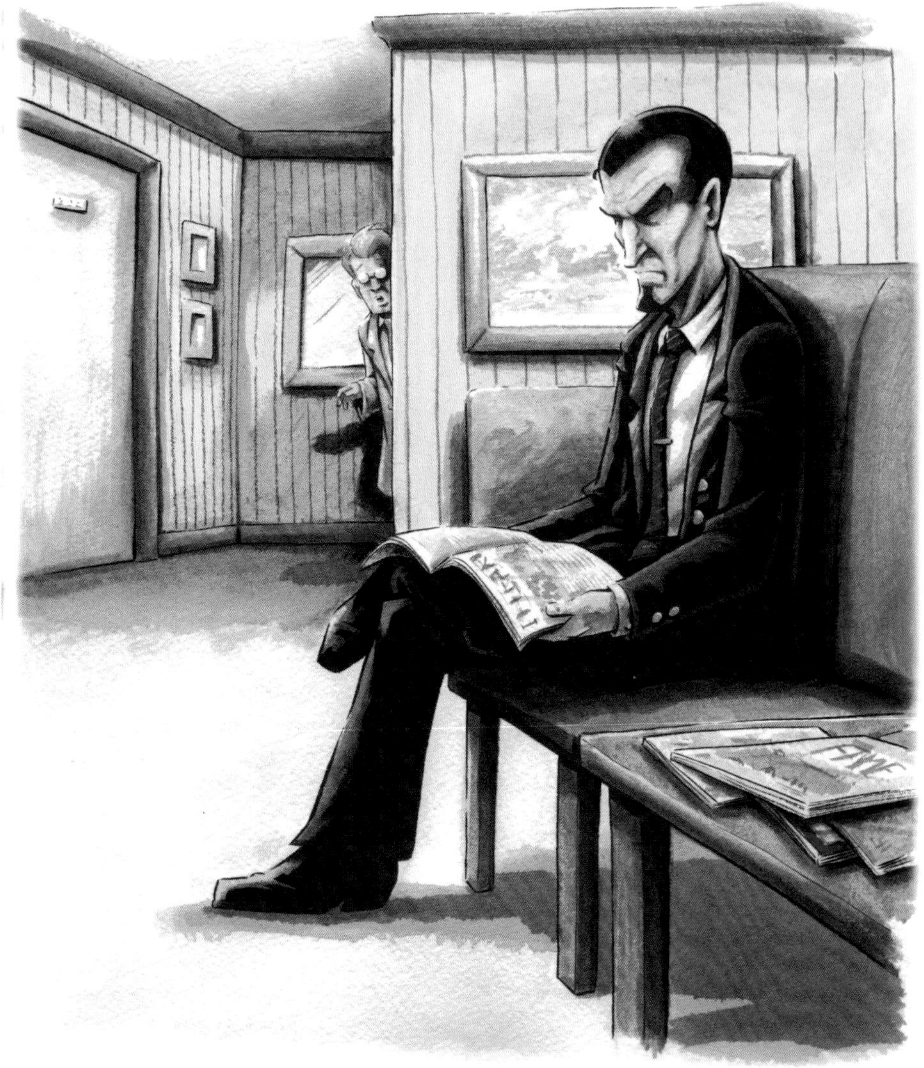

THEN...
38 YEARS EARLIER...

The two of them were 2600 feet above sea level when it happened. One of them heard it coming a split-second before the other did, and that's what saved their lives...His superior hearing.

It was three days later that they were found alive, buried under the rubble. She knew something was wrong when she woke up Christmas morning and they weren't there. She stayed back at base camp this year instead of joining them like she always had in years past. This year she was pregnant with their sixth, so she stayed back at the camp, helping with the cooking and other camp chores.

They'd been late before on other expeditions but never on Christmas. That's how she knew something was wrong. She was scared to leave the camp but had no choice, really, she had to go out and search for them.

She was grateful their other children were safe back home... Safe and sound back at the castle.

NOW...

Peter Valentine wasn't happy at all. He was extremely busy and having to have a dental examination wasn't exactly convenient right now. Christmas was just days away now; it was "crunch time" at Halcyon, their busiest time of the year. Additionally, there was a board meeting tomorrow to discuss first quarter projections for next year and then there was the big summit scheduled the day after. Peter chuckled at the idea of calling the meeting a "summit." It wasn't really a meeting of high-ranking government officials; it was more like them all gathering so that Halcyon could tell them what they were all going to do. Halcyon knew about the disappearance of Santa's body from the desert facility six months ago. They knew about it and were not happy at all. They just hadn't figured out yet who liberated him. Not that it mattered, really, to Peter. They had the castle now. Even if Santa were to try and recapture it he would fail. Especially now that they had huge armies amassed from over fifty different countries. They had The List, after all. And as long as they had that they were unstoppable. *Extortion is such a beautiful thing*, thought Peter. Yes, they had The List...safe and sound where nobody would find it. He personally saw to that. Even if, as he suspected, they had a "man on the inside" it wouldn't help. If anyone discovered its location and attempted to obtain it they'd be in for a *big* surprise.

Big and ugly, thought Peter as he sat in the waiting room. He chuckled softly to himself.

Norbie had no choice, he sent out the signal.

Randall hadn't expected it to hurt. Norbie told him to expect a "little buzzing sensation." This actually *hurt*. He supposed it had to. He had to send a strong signal to make sure Randall received it. But still!

"He's sent the signal," moaned Randall, "Norbie's found something."

"Is he in danger?!" asked Santa, concerned.

"I-I don't think so…it's a different signal."

Santa walked slowly back to the large chair and sat down. He was silent…deep in thought. Wondering what Norbie had discovered, frustrated, having no way of knowing that right now.

Randall approached him rubbing the right side of his face where the tooth was painfully buzzing. "Well, what are we going to do? We've got to do something!"

"I understand that," shot back Santa, "but we're not ready yet. We have no choice but to wait for the others to arrive. He's going to have to sit tight just a little bit longer." There was a long pause before Santa continued. "Let's just hope he doesn't do anything foolish in that time."

He wasn't sure what to do now. He could just send him away––cancel the appointment—but that might arouse suspicion. Especially after insisting on the examination the way he had. He could let one of the hygienists handle the exam, but again, that might look suspicious since he had always conducted the first examination himself. And Halcyon knew that; they commended him for it. No, he'd have to move forward. He had no choice.

He called Peter Valentine in for his examination.

THEN...
38 YEARS AGO...

When they had heard about the capturing of the castle and the death of Santa (for that is what they were told. That he was dead) the leaders of the world were terribly shocked. Not only for the fact that Santa was dead, but for the fact that Halcyon was actually able to pull this off. Immediate retaliation was suggested and discussed. A plan was made. This was one of the few times in the history of the world that the majority of world governments found themselves in almost complete agreement. Halcyon had to be stopped. With the might of the castle at their disposal they became a serious threat to the balance of world power—both militarily and economically. They would contact Halcyon and deliver their ultimatum: withdraw from the North Pole immediately or face the combined might of their armies.

But it was Halcyon who contacted them first. The message was simple. "We have The List."

There would have to be further discussions.

***

When the Elves that were stationed at the secret hubs around the world heard about the attack they were also shocked. The enormity of what had happened shocked and saddened them beyond comprehension. Their family and friends…most of them were there at the castle. All gone now. All dead. But they knew Santa wasn't dead. They knew because of the link that they shared with him. They were able to contact the Elves at the other hubs and form a plan of their own. And so they did.

***

After the rescue from the mountainside the three of them huddled by the warmth of the fire at the base camp retelling what had happened.

"It was a missile," said the one who had heard it just seconds before it had struck.

"But why? Who would fire upon us like that?" asked his burly companion.

"Oh my god!" shouted back the first. "The castle!"

And the three of them quickly gathered what they could and fled the mountainside.

NOW...

"Santa," said one of the Elves from the initial rescue team, "the first have arrived. They've broken through. The others are coming...they'll be here soon."

It was six days since Norbie had sent the signal. Their own signal had been sent weeks prior. And now the "gathering" would start.

It was a difficult matter to coordinate: Where to gather all the Elves that had been hiding all these years. There would be tens of thousands of them. But if they were to strike back against the armies now occupying the castle they had no choice but to call their own forces together. It was risky. Having them all in such close proximity left them vulnerable to an attack from Halcyon, but they had the element of surprise on their side. Santa had figured that Halcyon knew he was planning some kind of coup to recapture the castle, and were expecting it, but they didn't know when or that he had an army such as he had.

And so they came. In small contingents, leaving the majority of their individual groups back, away from Santa's makeshift headquarters.

If only Halcyon knew how close they were. But how could they, really? This was not their native land. It was native to no humans. This was the land of the Elves. Born there and privy to all this land's secrets.

"Well, I should get back before I'm missed," said Randall, "still gotta 'punch the clock.'"

And with that Randall McMahon left his small cottage where he resided in one of the southern villages on the outskirts of the North Pole. The cottage, like so many of the other cottages there, that had the "old tunnels" under them. The old underground network the Elves once used to move to and fro from the castle during the harshest of storms and the bitter colds. A network of tunnels *long* since abandoned (most collapsed) since they learned how to control the climate around the castle.

The old tunnels now "up and running" again—running under the entire planet's surface, in fact. Connecting the North Pole to all the secret hubs scattered far and wide.

It's amazing what forty thousand Elves can accomplish in thirty-eight years.

Yes, Santa and his rescuers had been there all along at the North Pole since his rescue…right under Halcyon's noses.

***

Randall punched in and went to work as supervisor of shipping and receiving like he had every day for the past few years. Doing nothing out of the ordinary—nothing to arouse any type of suspicion. He hadn't had any type of direct contact with Norbie in weeks. Every communication was done in a clandestine fashion. He had left the predetermined counter-signal the morning after Norbie sent his first signal. Randall's counter-signal was a simple one. The morning after the signal was sent Randall was to indicate whether or not he received it by simply leaving the third blind from the right of the front door of his cottage two/thirds closed while the others were all completely shut. No type of phone call, e-mail, or written message would be sent: too risky. They had long known that much of what went on at the castle was monitored by Halcyon. Even when Norbie placed the receiving device in Randall's tooth all of the instructions were written down on small pieces of notepaper, read, agreed upon, and then eaten so as never to be discovered. Nothing was ever spoken aloud.

Norbie must have seen Randall's counter-signal because shortly thereafter the buzzing in Randall's tooth returned. It was predetermined that if Norbie were to encounter any sort of trouble the first signal would be sent. One short, steady signal lasting about one minute in duration indicating something serious, or a pulsating signal of five seconds on five seconds off for one minute indicating immediate danger. Randall was relieved when he first received the signal that it didn't indicate the latter. Then, if Randall received it he would indicate so by sending a counter-signal of his own. Once Norbie saw this affirmation he would, once again, send a signal back to Randall; Again either one long, steady burst of one minute to indicate he received Randall's confirmation and that Randall should sit tight, or a pulsing signal in five-second bursts—five on, five off—for the one minute period, indicating that since the first signal was sent the danger levels had gone up. They couldn't risk it being any longer than a minute as there was the risk of the signal being picked up by Halcyon's detection devices. Again, Randall was relieved to receive the former signal rather than the latter. So, he would sit tight and see what happens next, relieved that his ally was in no apparent, immediate danger.

***

Peter didn't sense anything immediately. Not right away. The examination started and everything was going along fine. The dentist, Dr. Lember, seemed a capable employee, but was a bit quieter than he expected. From all the employee evaluations that he had read he had expected a more gregarious person. Perhaps this man was just intimidated by a superior. Peter did fancy himself something of an imposing figure.

So it was Peter who initiated the conversation.

"Well, how do they look?"

"E-Excuse me?" asked Norbie.

"My teeth…how do they *look?*"

"Oh…yes, of course," stammered Norbie, "they, um…so far they look fine."

"Never had a cavity in my life. Perfect teeth," bragged Peter.

After a couple minutes of silence—just some bland muzak and the soft clicks from the small dental tools the only sounds being heard—Peter continued, "So, what makes one want to become a Dentist?"

"Oh, uh, I don't know," Norbie replied. "I guess I've always wanted to be a Dentist."

Norbie said more, he continued on, but Peter wasn't listening anymore. He had found his "inside man." The Dentist. And he knew what he was after.

And so, Peter decided to give him what he wanted.

Norbie should have sent the signal with the five-second intervals and canceled the examination of Peter Valentine as soon as he saw him sitting there in the waiting room. That's what he should have done. But he didn't. Instead he proceeded with the exam.

It was going along well…the small talk just a bit uncomfortable. His words guarded. Norbie saw this as a chance…their chance. His chance. He knew that Peter Valentine had The List. He was certain. Now he had to figure out a way to find where he was hiding it.

So he played along making pleasant conversation. It was Peter who initiated it actually, asking benign questions, and that helped. He got the ball rolling. It seemed, at first, that Peter was in a hurry to get the exam over with, but since it started he had appeared to relax and wasn't in as much of a rush. Peter asked another question.

"So how long have you been with us?"

"Oh, this is my twenty-fifth year with Halcyon, actually," answered Norbie.

"Twenty-five years! You don't look that old," said Peter. "Twenty-five years…well that's quite an accomplishment," he continued. "A landmark like that—a model employee such as yourself—I really admire the way you stayed on me about getting this exam, by the way…showed gumption! All that shouldn't go unnoticed…unrewarded."

Norbie started to say something—that any type of *reward*

was certainly unnecessary—but stopped himself, wanting to see where this might lead.

"I tell you what," continued Peter, "give my secretary a call this afternoon and we'll set something up. Have you ever toured the inside of the castle?"

"No," lied Norbie, actually excited. He had, of course, many decades past when he worked making the toys, but things had changed since Halcyon's occupation, and very few were now allowed inside the main gates. "That would be an honor."

Peter continued, "I'll give you a tour, take you to lunch…" He paused for effect, Norbie never noticing that he was being baited, "…you've heard of the book, right?"

Yes! Norbie thought to himself, *This is it!* but replied, "Book? …what book?" playing it coy.

Peter played along, "The List."

Norbie feigned shock and delight, "Th-The List!?! Why… Yes!…Yes, of course."

"Would you like to see it?" Peter asked. "It's really quite something."

"Of course, sir. That-That would be wonderful!" Norbie couldn't believe his good luck.

"We'll set it up." *Hook, line and sinker*, Peter thought to himself as he lie there waiting for the examination to end.

***

He was hungry. They kept him that way. Hungry and cold. They told him things as well. That he was abandoned…that they were all dead…that if he wanted to eat then he would have

96

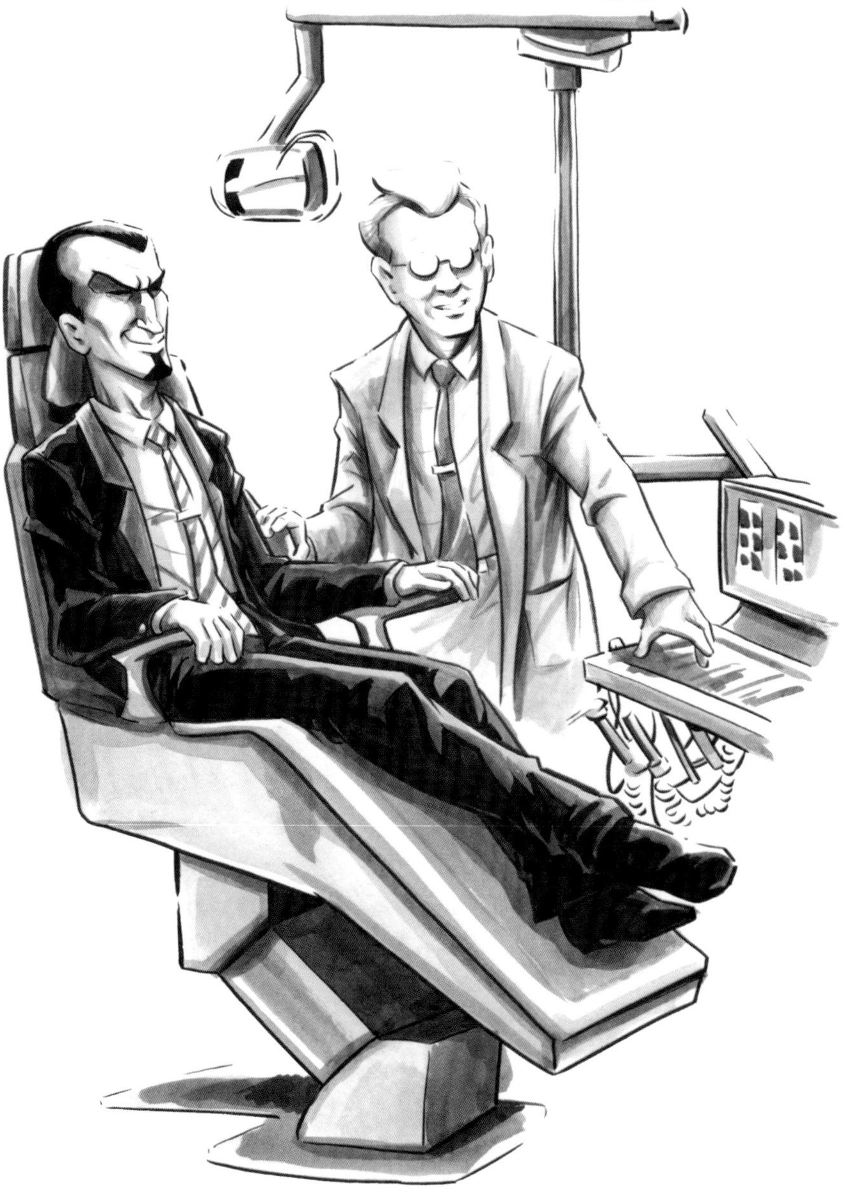

to listen...to do as he was told.
He was hungry...so he did.

***

They were waiting. Millions of them. Tens of millions of them. Their voices all but whispers in the wind. But soon it would be the eve of the Holy Day...and their voices would thunder.

***

"We're running out of time!"

"But we haven't heard back yet from Norbie!" protested Randall.

"We can't wait any longer!" Santa replied back. "It's only three days until Christmas Eve."

Santa motioned to the Elves standing near the doorway. They quickly ran off. They would signal the others to commence the attack. They could wait no longer.

"Come on, Norbie..." Randall whispered softly to himself.

***

He swung the great axe as hard as he could…over and over and over again. Taking massive chunks of ice out of the endless wall in front of them. Those with him watched in awe. Seeing this man, a mere mortal, swing the axe as if he were a god. He said nothing as he worked. He just kept swinging his axe. Over and over and over again.

***

The tour was fantastic; Norbie was truly impressed with the changes made by Halcyon. Almost everything was automated now. Computer consoles and massive machinery were everywhere. White plastic, shiny metal and sparkling glass. Everything was spotless…spotless and sanitized. It was, indeed, impressive, but it left Norbie with an empty feeling––the thought of what all this extraordinary machinery had replaced.

The lunch was also magnificent. Norbie was treated to a seven-course meal in the company of the Board of Halcyon. They dined on lobster, prime rib, caviar, fresh fruits and mouth-watering desserts. Norbie was stuffed. After lunch he was treated to an hour in the company spa where he was massaged, manicured and steamed nearly to the point where, normally, he would have drifted away in dreamy slumber had it not been for the mission at hand. The entire morning's festivities lasted nearly three hours. And now they were here…The Chamber. The heavily guarded room that held The List.

Norbie entered the Chamber with Peter—just the two of

them. The plan was to merely locate The List so that when the attack came they'd know where it was and hopefully retrieve it. Back in Santa's hands the armies of the other countries would hopefully change sides and the tide of the battle would turn. That was the plan. Trying to retrieve it now would be next to impossible; the room was too heavily guarded and monitored by security devices. No, Norbie's mission was a simple one; locate The List. Nothing heroic.

That was the plan…"Plan A."

They entered the Chamber alone. Norbie heard something inside…something moving…something…breathing?

"Oh!...*OH, NO!"* Norbie screamed when he saw what was inside. He caught one last glimpse of Peter standing out in the hallway smiling, holding The List, before the doors slid completely shut between them.

Norbie bit down hard on the false tooth in the back of his mouth sending out that final staccato signal. The last signal he would send before his horrible death.

Norbie's last signal came as Randall stood by Santa's side looking at something he'd thought only existed in storybooks. Again it was encoded and sent through the device in Randall's tooth. This was the one-minute signal consisting of short, staccato bursts—The one indicating urgency. At the end of the one minute, it was strange, but Randall could have sworn he also heard something else...*Voices?*

***

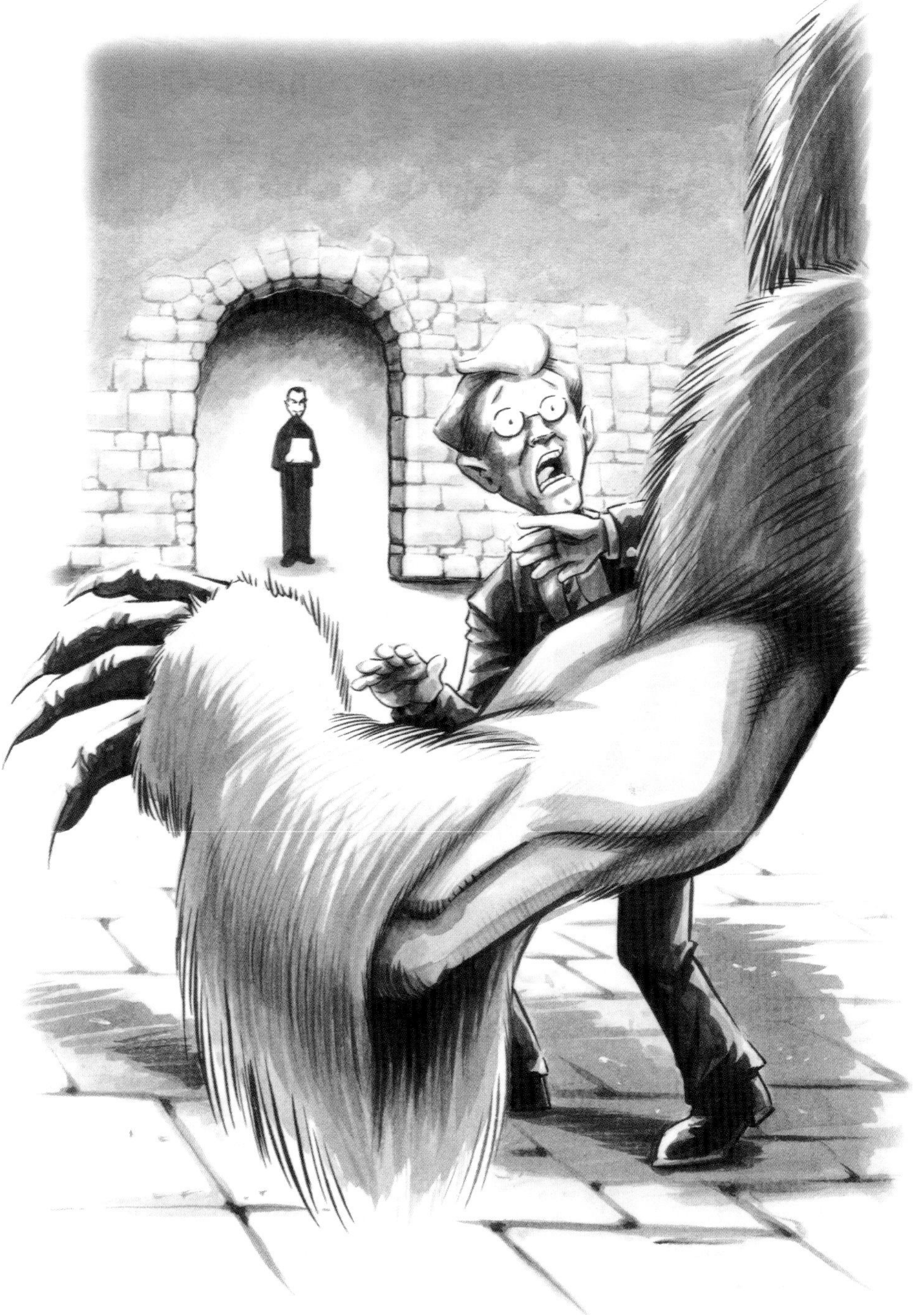

It was one of the Elves who came running in with it. This was an Elf in charge of one of the distribution hubs located in South America—one of the Argentina hubs. The Elf holding the package was accompanied by four larger, sturdier Elves. Bodyguards. He handed the package to Santa. The outer wrapper was plain brown paper, but inside was a beautiful, ornately jeweled box. A hat box.

"Hello, old friend," said Santa opening the lid of the beautiful box. He took out the hat and laid it gently upon the icy ground of the tunnel floor. He chanted words that were thousands of years old and that only he and the Elves understood.

And although Randall didn't understand the words, he felt the tingling static sensation the words seemed to create in the air, raising the hair on his arms and the back of his neck.

The figure rose up from out of the icy ground before them––a whirlwind of ice and snow whipping around it. Massive. Towering over all but Santa. It spoke. And when it did the air seemingly dropped another ten degrees.

"My liege." It spoke through clenched teeth, its voice an icy, breathy whisper—The anger palpable. But it was clear whom the anger was directed towards. Not Santa. No, Santa was his oldest, dearest friend. Their affection for each other was a bond only shared by the closest of brothers. Unbreakable. Its anger was for those who destroyed him. Those who obliterated him in the attack, leaving nothing but the battered hat lying at the gates of the stormed castle along with the corpses of the fallen. Left for dead. It was one of the few fleeing reindeer that managed to gather up the hat in its teeth and escape with it. But he lie dormant all these years, trapped by the magician's incantations—the mage who first created him so many decades past—the magical shackles that only his brother could unloose. And his brother lie trapped as well in the hard desert floor. Held by the shackles of another magician.

Santa put his hand on the shoulder of his brother. Lesser beings would have experienced painful frostbite upon touching the sub-zero shoulder, but not Santa. He smiled at his long-lost comrade and softly whispered the simple name the children had chosen for him.

"IceCap."

"Sorry," interrupted Randall, "but I'm getting another signal from Norbie. I think he's in trouble!"

Santa looked from his long-lost friend to Randall with concern. "Let's move," was all that he said.

As they quickly moved down the icy tunnel, the cold, hollow voice of *IceCap of the Hoarfrost Men* was heard asking, "That *dentist* kid? What's he been up to?"

***

Peter spoke to the generals of the foreign armies, steeling them for the attack that would soon come. He knew it would come on the Eve of the Holy day, Christmas. Of course it would. When else? They may have thought this would come as something of a surprise to Halcyon, but it wouldn't. It mattered little either way. There was simply no way on Earth Santa could attack the castle and have any chance of winning. Halcyon's armies were massive.

The foreign generals were uncomfortable with the war they were about to engage in. But, as is often the case in matters of war, they had their orders. They were soldiers, and soldiers followed orders. The politicians fought about whether the fight was just or not, the soldiers just fought it. And so they listened to this man, Peter Valentine: Mouthpiece of Halcyon: Halcyon the country, Halcyon the corporation. Money. Halcyon was

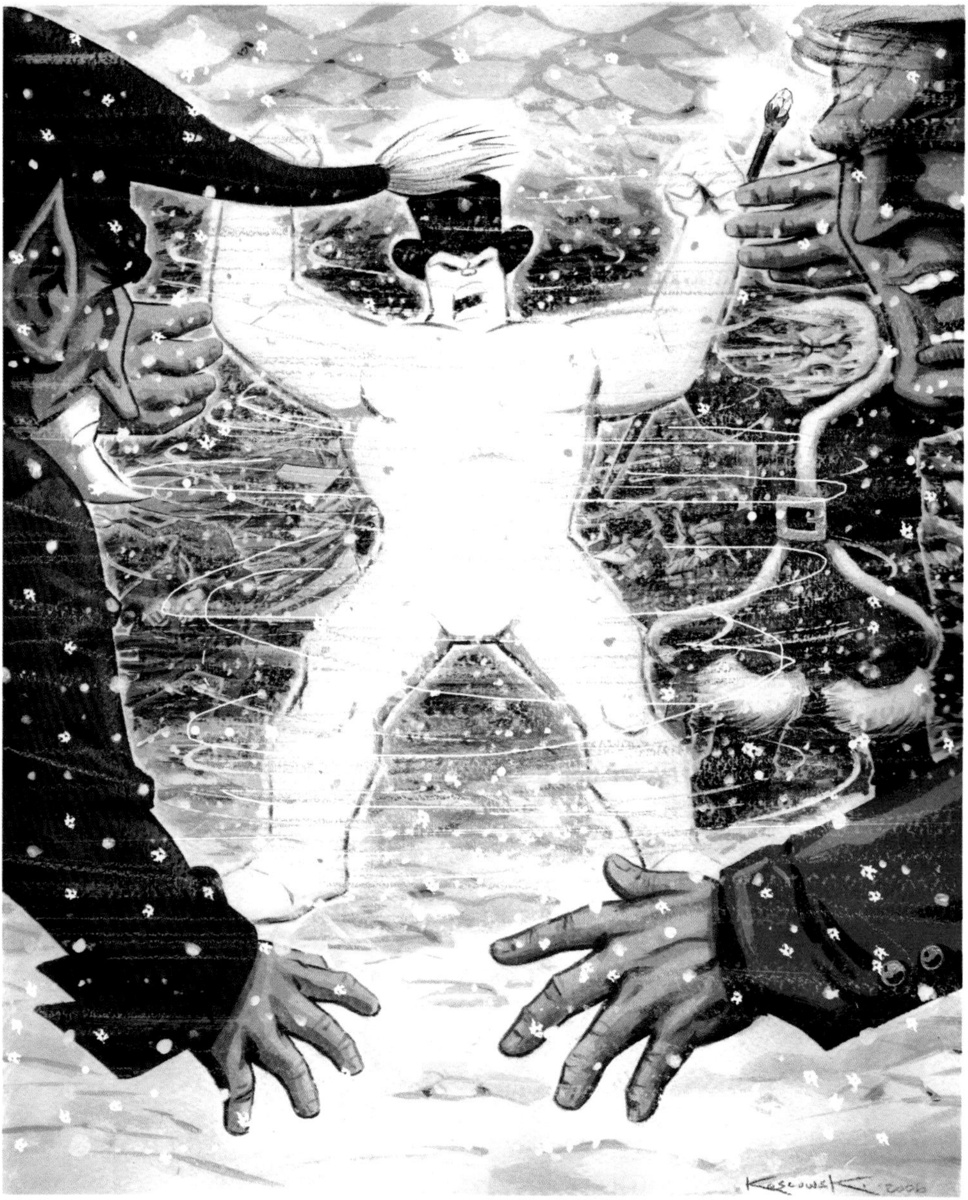

money. These generals knew that. They knew that, once again, they were fighting for money. They knew of The List and its powers—the hold Halcyon had over their respective leaders—but they also knew that in addition to the threats—the extortion—there were bribes and payoffs as well. Their leaders didn't just do this out of self-preservation. They weren't merely cowards. They did it for money as well.

No, they weren't just cowards, they were *greedy* cowards.

THEN...
38 YEARS AGO...

"It's simple, really," Peter Valentine told them all, "just leave us be. Let us do our work."

The world leaders were all gathered there thirty-eight years ago...Those that mattered, anyways...those with power. An emergency meeting there at the United Nations building to hear the "terms" from Halcyon after their occupation of the North Pole. Peter Valentine spoke to them from a large view-screen via closed-circuit transmission sent from their new headquarters.

"You will refrain from interfering, and, in return, *we* will not interfere with *you*." Peter said this all with an almost winsome lilt in his voice—a wry smile on his face.

"Choose to interfere and there will be...consequences. We will be watching you." Peter held up the book as he said this last part. The List.

That was it...end of meeting. The message was received loud and clear. And over the course of the next few decades, while Santa lie buried beneath the desert floor, the leaders of the world's countries did, indeed, look the other way while the postcards arrived. They let Halcyon operate without any interference and Halcyon let them be as well.

And in that time Halcyon amassed power and wealth beyond imagining.

NOW...
CHRISTMAS EVE DAY...

Santa and his team led the frontal attack on the castle. He was accompanied by Randall and the team of Elves that freed him from the desert. All told there were twenty-six of them.

They stood there facing an army of thousands.

Defiantly, Santa demanded their surrender, "LAY DOWN YOUR ARMS AND NONE SHALL BE HARMED! SURRENDER!"

The armies of Halcyon stood there, motionless. No reply was made. Santa's small force echoed Halcyon's silence. The silence lasted for several minutes until finally a small disturbance could be seen amongst the Halcyon troops. A ripple seemed to slowly move from the back of the formation, near the castle gates, up towards the front lines of the troops. Something was slowly moving towards them.

It was a man being pushed in a wheelchair. It was Sir Stephen T. Carlson, still impossibly alive after all these years. Well past one hundred now and just a shriveled up shell of the man he used to be. All sorts of diabolical looking tubes and bags hung about him, the soft beeping sounds of the various boxes and lights being heard. His back a painful looking hump, his head, crooked, hung down low. His red-rimmed eyes were cloudy with cataracts—barely visible below his brow—straining upward to see.

Amazingly, he spoke; it was little more than a scratchy whisper. "I am Sir Stephen T. Carlson, President of Halcyon… These are Halcyon's grounds that you trespass upon… You are under arrest."

Santa spoke again, "THIS IS *MY* HOME THAT YOU OCCUPY *ILLEGALLY!* I HAVE COME TO RECLAIM IT. SURRENDER IT NOW AND YOU SHALL ALL RECEIVE FAIR TRIALS!"

Sir Stephen sat motionless in his chair for some time. They could see his lips moving then some minutes later, but could not hear what he said. The one who accompanied him, the short one in the cloak who had pushed his chair, bent over to listen to him. Randall thought it funny that he hadn't noticed the man before just now. Why hadn't he noticed him? He stole a quick glance at Santa. Was he wrong, or did Santa look momentarily confused as well?

Before he could give it any further thought, this man spoke, and when he did all Hell broke loose.

***

They broke up through the sub-basement's floor just in time to see their friend disappear in to the massive jaws of the great beast. Too late.

"NOOO!" screamed the one with the axe. "NOOOOOO!..."

The Great Beast quickly jerked its head towards the annoying sound. This wasn't the screaming it had just ended from the other one…the little one. This annoying sound was coming from a different one…a bigger one.

It looked…*familiar* to the beast somehow.

"NORBIE!" the big one screamed now while running at him.

Norbie? It thought. That was somehow familiar to it, too. The big one was screaming something else as well, also familiar to the beast. The words tickled at the back of its brain, stimulating memories long lain dormant within it. A name?

"A-Bomb!" was what the big one was shouting. A-Bomb? *"A-Bomb! NOOO! How could you?!"*

The name—A-Bomb—caused the beast to hesitate just for a moment—just long enough for the big one to barge headfirst into its side knocking it over. The chains that held the beast prevented it from being thrown too far—they also caused the beast and its attacker to become entangled. The beast had

its attacker now. It was furious! It wrapped one of its chains around this screaming large one's throat. It began to squeeze. A choking sound came from its attacker.

"A-A-Bomb..." the big one said weakly, "A-Bomb...it's me! *Klondike!"*

Klondike? A-Bomb? Norbie? What were these words?...These ...names? It felt the big one struggling less now... *Klondike...*

Klondike? KLONDIKE!!

His friend…Klondike Saskatchewan! The great prospector! He remembered again! It was Klondike and this other little one…Norbie, that liberated him…saved him from himself so many years ago…a horrible life filled with death and terror… loneliness…he remembers they stopped him once before from eating another friend!...A different friend...who was that? No matter…he remembered Klondike again and he remembered Norbie. He remembered them welcoming him into their band of outcasts…misfits. How they all became a part of Santa's family. He remembered the funny name this man called him again now as well. He was A-Bomb! Yes, they were friends. Great friends! It was the one in black…the one who always hurt him who wasn't his friend!

***

"Hello, my name is Peter Valentine, CEO of Halcyon." He smiled, looking directly at Santa now. "Of course that was not always the name by which I went."

"Black Peter!" snarled Santa.

"Yes, there was that one," Peter Valentine cooed. "Still my favorite I think."

He directed his gaze at Randall now. "Ahh…Mr. McMahon… I wouldn't have suspected you. Interesting. I see that you are somewhat confused. Perhaps you didn't realize that I had a previous relationship with your Mr. Claus.

"I worked for him many years ago. Many, many years ago. Until I was deemed…unnecessary."

"You were a sadistic maniac," spat Santa.

"*I was* exactly *as I was supposed to be!*"

"What's going on?" asked Randall.

No one answered at first. They just stared at each other. Santa looking grim and Black Peter with that same wry smile looking back. Finally Santa responded.

"He is my greatest shame. That is who he is. Black Peter. Few remember him and that is as it should be." He paused again before continuing, "It was Black Peter's job to frighten the bad children—"

"Frighten?" interrupted Black Peter with a chuckle.

Again Santa was reticent with his reply. "Punish," he said at last.

"Punish?" questioned Randall.

"I whipped them." Black Peter said with a smile. "We traveled together."

Santa winced at this. Silent as Black Peter continued.

"He would deliver the goodies to the good little boys and girls, and while he did that I would go into the rooms of the bad little boys and girls, get out my whip and—"

"Enough!" shouted Santa. *"That was a long time ago! "*

"Yes. A long time ago. And then one day you told me I wasn't necessary any more. My methods…outdated."

"Times change, Peter."

"Oh, is it *Peter* now? "

"What do you want?"

"It *was* Peter, you know?" He directed this to Randall again. "I was simply *Peter the Elf.* One of Santa's *top* Elves. He handpicked me for the job. Called me *Black Peter*. Said it would scare the kids better. It worked."

Randall looked at Santa in disbelief. Wanting Santa to call this nutcase out as a fraud. Debunk his story. Say it wasn't true. Santa's not looking at Randall but continuing to lock his gaze upon Black Peter was answer enough. The story was true.

"My God!" whispered Randall.

"Oh yes," said Black Peter, "and he had hoped that over time I would be forgotten. He secreted me away, kept me locked up tight. His own personal little *'Fallen Angel.'* And people did forget about me. Most of them anyways." He put his hands on the shoulders of Sir Stephen as he said this.

Could it be? Thought Randall. *Could Sir Stephen have been one of Black Peter's victims? How old was he?!*

"But I didn't forget," continued Black Peter. "I sat there and sat there and thought more and more on how I would someday get back at him. You can actually learn quite a lot about yourself while sitting in a jail cell you know.

"For instance, did you know that Elves are great at concealing themselves? Oh yes, centuries and centuries of self-preservation. A natural defense mechanism honed by hundreds of years of practice and augmented by just a titch of magick.

"I worked on that while I sat there."

Randall now understood why he hadn't noticed this man pushing the wheelchair.

"I was amazed myself the day I simply up and walked away. My keepers didn't even seem to notice…All but forgotten." He stared at Santa again.

"I *never* forgot," said Santa.

"And I think that's all that kept me alive. Thanks! If you'd have forgotten me as well, then I'd have completely faded away. Gods die when they're forgotten. Sir Stephen here didn't forget about me either. I found him…remembered him. He remembered me, too. His fear made me strong again. We've been keeping each other strong for a long time now."

"You're *not* a god," said Santa.

"Not yet." Black Peter nodded at his generals. "Kill them."

Black Peter's armies quickly formed ranks around him, shielding him and Sir Stephen. They formed a line and prepared to open fire upon Santa and his small band of troops. Santa thrust his arms skyward, a long staff in his right hand. The jeweled staff lit up at its end and the light shone upward.

A beacon!

As if on cue they fell from the sky! Without a sound! Hundreds of them! Darting this way and that almost too quickly for the eye to see. And they dropped things into the armed forces of

Halcyon. They were bombs. Flying Reindeer dropping bombs––Nothing mystical or magickal about it.

The Halcyon troops were caught completely off-guard. There was a moment of panic as they fired wildly into the night sky. Thousands of weapons were fired up into the air— very few finding their actual targets. But fall some of the mighty Reindeer did, becoming weapons once again, and for the final time, navigating their dying forms into the heart of the enemy as the Kamikaze pilots would do. If still armed their impact was tremendous, if unarmed their horns their bayonets.

Santa then shot his arms out to his sides. Another signal. This time the hills themselves came alive upon seeing it. Tens of thousands of Elves rose up from under the snow where they lie hidden, waiting in the tunnels below. They charged forward.

"Masters of concealment," Black Peter whispered with a smile. "Very well done." He slipped back further from the battle, retreating with Sir Stephen towards the castle. Inside the castle he would be safe from harm. The castle's defenses were, after all, impenetrable.

Klondike pulled again, harder this time. The Abominable Snowman emptied the contents of his stomach at last.

"Never thought I'd see the day I'd be a doin' the Heimlich on an A-Bomb!" bellowed Klondike Saskatchewan.

There on the cold concrete floor lie Norbie the dentist, not moving. They all moved in closer on him. One of the Elves that dug through with Klondike asked if he was dead.

"Course he ain't dead!" shouted Klondike. "He's an Elf ain't he?" And he proceeded to poke Norbie with the end of his pick-axe.

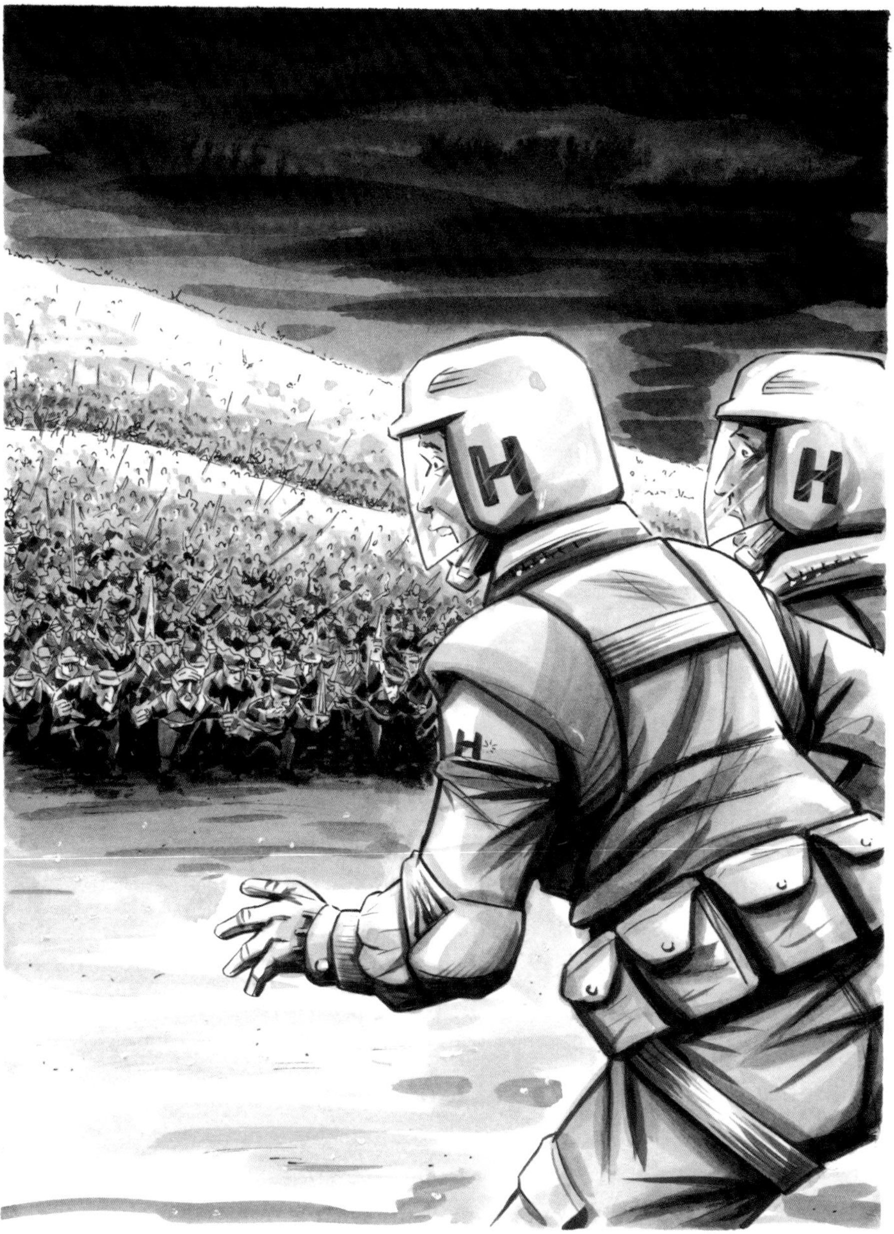

"'Sides, the A-Bomb ain't got no teeth!" With this the beast smiled almost sheepishly and Norbie slowly stirred to life.

"He was…*ahyuck*…my first…extraction," Norbie coughed out.

"See! I told ya! Fit as a fiddle!" Klondike exclaimed proudly. He quickly turned to help Norbie up off the floor before the others could see the tear roll down his cheek.

"Now let's go find out who done this ta A-Bomb!" shouted Klondike.

"I know who did it," said Norbie.

The sound of the Abominable Snowman roaring could be heard down the many corridors of the castle. The troops advancing on The Chamber heard it as they approached, summoned by the Chamber's detection devices. Many knew from the terrible sound that they wouldn't survive this day.

***

Elves can die. They are very long-lived—nearly immortal—but they do die. Many thousands died the day that Halcyon first invaded the North Pole and many thousands died this day as well. Their initial attack did manage to catch the Halcyon armies off-guard, allowing them to inflict some significant damage to the Halcyon troops, but only momentarily. Thousands were slaughtered as the first volley of missiles was launched. Armed with only their sturdy warrior frames and basic Elven weapons they were hopelessly outmatched. The castle had always held the bulk of their most sophisticated, most powerful weaponry, and now it was being used against them. But still they fought and fought proudly. They fought with their King at their side. Together they pushed against the Halcyon hordes deep into the thick of them. Halcyon's generals were pleased as they now had Santa's army surrounded: the air attack also under control, the reindeer being beaten back by their air forces.

***

From within the castle walls Black Peter oversaw the battle, instructing his generals inside the castle's "War Room;" a cavernous room filled with many desks, chairs, computers, monitors and the people operating them. He watched with pleasure as his hated enemy's troops fell before his eyes. But still *he* would not fall. Black Peter saw him hit over and over again by the bullets and grenades and walk through it all unscathed. Black Peter sighed. *What would they do with him this time,* he wondered. *Maybe launching him into space wasn't such a bad idea after all.* He chuckled softly. They couldn't do it thirty-eight years ago because they didn't have the budget, but that certainly didn't factor in now, did it? *Yes,* he decided, *after we kill all of his little army this time, we'll just have to launch him out into space. How delightful.*

***

It was almost as if all was lost when Santa again motioned with his mighty staff. This time pulling it in towards himself and uttering the words Randall and the others heard down in the tunnels. Again the winds swirled and the static electricity charged the air. Santa pulled the hat from the inside of his heavy coat, hidden no more—an ace in the hole. He had waited until he was in the thick of them to let his brother's wrath loose! He held the hat out in front of him and dropped it to the frozen ground. This time the icy ground was also covered with the blood of the fallen—the blood of IceCap's comrades. He arose with their blood a part of him now—adding to his power—the bright red blood visibly seen pulsing through his snow-white form. He looked terrifying!

"My God!" Whispered Randall, his eyes wide with wonder. "He-He's so…The shows I watched when I was a boy were—"

"Fairytales!" an elf finished for him. "Kid's stories! This ain't no fairytale…no TV show…this is the real thing!"

IceCap tore through the troops with unbridled savagery. They couldn't stop him, their bullets useless. The grenades that stopped him so many years before were also rendered useless with Santa so near. Empowered by the close proximity to his magickal Brother, IceCap's wounds would instantaneously regenerate. When blown apart the millions of frozen particles would swirl furiously about in the air, the hat suspended, and his form rematerialize, still marching forward, never missing a beat! He pummeled through the troops literally breaking them into frozen bits and pieces—freezing and pummeling them at the same time. Dozens of them fell. Soon it would be hundreds. The tide momentarily turned.

IceCap didn't notice the flamethrowers flanking him from behind.

**

Klondike, Norbie, A-Bomb and the small band of Elves easily vanquished the Halcyon troops sent to handle them. It was the Abominable Snowman that took the lead and inflicted the most damage. Inside the halls of the castle the Halcyon troops were limited in the weapons they could effectively use, and the angry beast quickly tore through them.

"We've got to get up to the High Tower," said Norbie, "that's where Black Peter will be. That's where the War Room is." Norbie had by this time explained who Black Peter was to the others. Every time he mentioned his name A-Bomb would roar with rage.

"We need a diversion or something, though, or we'll never get up there undetected."

"I ever tell ya 'bout the time I was buried on the side of a mountain?!" asked Klondike.

Outside, right in the middle of the pitched battle, Santa handed Randall a pair of goggles. "You better put these on," was all that he said.

"Sir, they've taken out squads twenty-six and seven and are headed our way. They've breached the security doors on level three."

Black Peter saw them as well. He was watching them on the monitors. "They won't get far," he said, pointing to a different monitor showing a larger contingent of very heavily armed Halcyon troops hunkered down in a corridor. They were waiting for Norbie and his friends.

He was about to continue. To say that even if they somehow miraculously managed to get past that troop that the booby-traps set up on level four would obliterate them, but he never got the chance. For all at once the room went red!

It was the red light. Even under tons of rubble she could see it shining through. That's how his wife found them thirty-eight years ago.

"Yep, buried alive!" continued Klondike to Norbie. "'Cover yer eyes' was what he said!" He motioned for Norbie and the others to do the same now, and he pressed a button on his wristwatch. "Cover yer eyes."

RED! The whole world went red! The Halcyon troops were bathed in it. Blinded by it! And the monitors inside the War Room were lit up so brightly that those inside were also blinded by it! It was that bright.

He couldn't have waited any longer, anyways. He knew he had to follow the plan but it was excruciating watching his

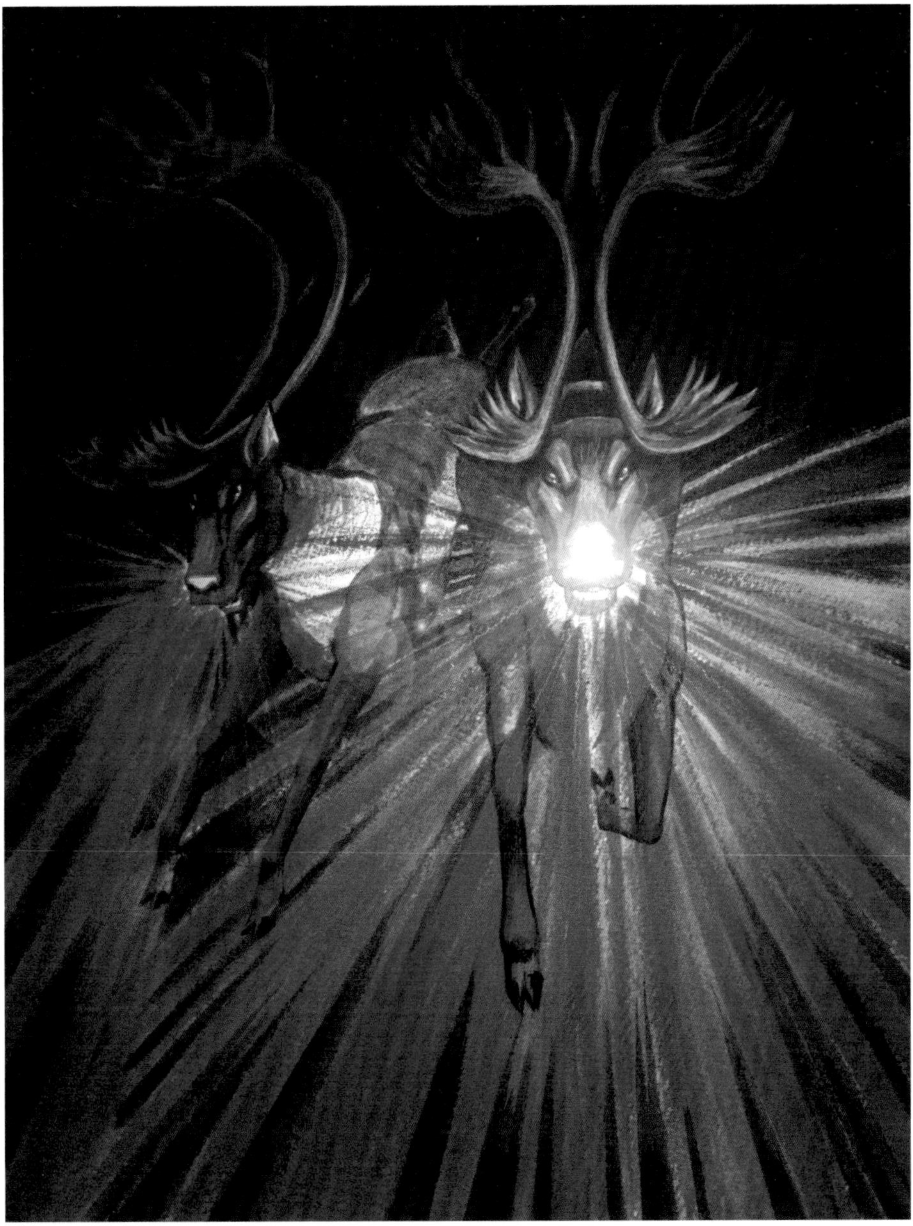

friends cut down while he just sat there. Waiting. And then he saw them setting up the flamethrowers, flanking them from their backside and he decided he could wait no longer. To Hell with the plan! He wouldn't watch any more of them die. But then, mercifully, Klondike's signal came! *Thank God*, he thought as he stood up from his hiding place.

"LET'S GO!" shouted Rendor—*Rendor The Red-Rider! Rendor the Magnificent*—and the two hiding with him came out as well. It was his wife, Klaaretteta, and their son, Donner— —Donner the second, named after The Red-Rider's father, now dead. Slain in the attack by Halcyon so many years ago. It was Donner the second now, The Red-Rider and Klaaretteta's only surviving child—their other five children were also killed along with the original Donner that horrible day.

They flew down into the battle and the sight of it was as magnificent as it was impossible. The Red-Rider and Donner II…Father and son: the son also born with his father's wonderful, glorious gift. The gift of the living light!

It shone brighter than they had ever shone it before. So bright it was that it seemed to pass right through things, encompassing all.

Randall McMahon had seen some amazing things in the last six months, but this took the cake. "Thanks for the glasses," was all he could manage as he looked to the sky. Even with them on he had to squint.

"SYSTEMS DOWN! ALL SYSTEMS DOWN!" was what Black Peter kept hearing. The surveillance systems were overloaded. All the screens went black—mercifully for their eyes. But now they were left in the dark—literally and metaphorically. They could no longer monitor the battle from a safe distance. Nor could they monitor the interior of the castle. They had two choices: remain there blind or leave and join the battle.

Black Peter looked to the others and said, "GO! Lead your troops on the field!" He smiled then, continuing, "We'll stay here…" he gestured to Sir Stephen, "and wait for the dentist!"

***

Norbie and the others passed through the corridors unobstructed now—the soldiers all apparently joining the battle outside. They cautiously entered the cavernous War Room and saw him calmly waiting there for them.

***

The tide of the battle turned again when The Red-Rider and Donner II joined the fray. Santa guided his ground forces toward the castle gates; The Red-Rider and the other reindeer commanded the sky.

"TAKE THE GATES!" shouted Santa.

The outer gates to the castle were where Halcyon's army made its final stand. There they now stood with all the castle's mighty arsenal at their disposal. The generals down alongside the ground troops now ready to fight. They had no choice, really. Black Peter still had The List.

***

He held The List as he sat there. Held it in his lap. Sir Stephen. Black Peter was nowhere in sight.

Norbie, Klondike, A-Bomb and the small band of Elves walked slowly into the room. Norbie was the one to break the silence.

"Where's Black Peter?"

There was no reply; the only response the hollow hissing sound and faint beeps from the machine that breathed for Sir Stephen.

Norbie approached Sir Stephen, sitting there in his chair, slack-jawed...*Asleep?* He walked up slowly and reached toward the book lying in Sir Stephen's lap.

The sound of the whip cracking was almost as loud as the scream now coming from Norbie's mouth. Norbie fell to his knees holding the bloody right hand that now had two less fingers on it.

From the dark recesses he appeared, seemingly at one with the shadows— flowing out from the blackness as if a part of it...connected. He was rolling up the whip while walking towards them. As always, he was smiling.

"Ooohhh my little dentist friend... you've been a bad, bad boy! For *shame*! Were you going to take Sir Stephen's book without even asking? Tsk tsk! I do believe that's *stealing!*"

He chuckled then and continued, "It's a good thing for you that I was here, however...Had you removed the book?...*Ka-Blooey!*" As Black Peter said this he mimed the explosion with his hands.

A-Bomb roared again, the sound

deafening. He advanced towards Black Peter. Black Peter shot him a glance while clenching his whip out in front of him. A-Bomb stopped, frozen in his tracks. Black Peter still had a hold on him.

"And you've been a bad boy, as well now, haven't you?"

The Abominable Snowman cowered, whimpering softly.

Klondike and the Elves were between Black Peter and the Abominable Snowman now, their backs towards the door through which they came. The door that was now sealed shut. Norbie was back behind Black Peter still kneeling on the ground beside Sir Stephen.

Black Peter advanced towards the Abominable snowman. "But you're going to be a good boy now again and listen, aren't you?

"Yes," he looked up at the beast, smiling, "you're going to listen to me now!" Black Peter looked from the cowering face of the beast now to his friends standing behind him. He kept on smiling.

***

Klaaretteta left as soon as Rendor and Donner flew off. She couldn't fly like her husband and son—she wasn't blessed with that wonderful gift—but she could run...very fast. She was one of Santa's magickal creatures after all. So she ran—as fast as she could—but not away from the battle. No, she ran towards it. The bastards inside that castle were the ones that murdered her children. She'd be damned if she let them kill another!

***

There was a momentary standoff on the battlefield as Santa's troops gathered, preparing to storm the gates. The Halcyon troops also stood, bracing for the attack. They were outnumbered now, but still had the castle as their stronghold. Santa knew this. He knew that if the battle continued to go against the Halcyon troops as it had that they would fall back into the castle and regroup. Once inside the battle would become a drawn out affair—his army's chances of winning doubtful. He wanted to end this now. He *needed* to end this now, he had no choice, it was almost midnight—less than a half hour to go. He *had* to be inside the castle before midnight struck. Santa stood up on the burnt out husk of a Halcyon tank. He shouted to the Halcyon troops.

"ONCE AGAIN I ASK YOU TO STAND DOWN! LAY DOWN YOUR ARMS AND SURRENDER! THERE HAS BEEN ENOUGH BLOODSHED FOR ONE DAY!"

He waited for their response.

Randall heard the voices again—the ones he thought he had heard before…when Norbie sent his last signal.

***

As Santa was preparing to ask for the Halcyon troops' surrender, the scene up above them in the castle would build to its dramatic conclusion.

"First the large one and his little Elf friends, and then the dentist. I want him to watch first," sneered Black Peter. "And this time rip the little bastard apart before swallowing him you big, toothless idiot!"

A-Bomb advanced upon Klondike and the Elves. He was

moaning and tears rolled down his big face, but he advanced nonetheless. Decades of torture conditioned the poor creature to obey the one who held the whip. The great beast hated this little creature in black, but he feared him even more. He didn't want to be hurt anymore.

"A-Bomb, stop!" pleaded Klondike. "What're ya doin'?! We're yer friends!"

He hesitated. He loved this big loud man…He *was* his friend. He didn't want to hurt him. He heard the little one in black shouting at him again. He felt the sting of the little one's whip upon his back. It hurt! But the pain inside his head was worse! He didn't know what to do!

But Klondike Saskatchewan did know what to do. He hurled his mighty pick-axe with a speed that belied his massive form, impaling it into the chest of Black Peter!

Black Peter screamed and dropped to the floor. But he somehow managed to hold the whip. No surprise, really, as it was almost a physical extension of himself.

Four of the Elves quickly ran for him. One lost his head before he took three steps, the other three dropped seconds thereafter. Even from his knees Black Peter proved deadly.

Norbie still knelt there by Sir Stephen. He stood up as quickly as he could now, straining, using the arm of Sir Stephen's chair to help him. He began talking to Sir Stephen as the others fought nearby, making quick use of the distraction.

"I think it's time for one last examination, boss," he managed, as he slowly opened Sir Stephen's mouth, his right hand shaking and bloody.

Little did Black Peter realize that Norbie wasn't, in fact, reaching *for* The List earlier...That it was *exactly* where he wanted it to be.

15 MINUTES TILL MIDNIGHT...

It was fifteen minutes from midnight now and the standoff still stood between Santa's army and the armies of Halcyon.

"I need to be inside the castle for this to work," Santa said to those around him. It was Randall, The fabled Red-Rider and his equally mighty son Donner II, a handful of Elf warriors and the mighty IceCap of the Hoarfrost Men.

"Maybe we can backtrack to my cottage and use Klondike's tunnel," suggested Randall.

"We're out of time," said Santa.

"Get on," it was Donner, "I'll get you in from above."

"NO!" shouted The Red-Rider, "It's too dangerous this close to the castle! The castle's defenses are just too strong!"

There was a moment of silence then. All present knew that this was the only way. They were out of time and they had no other choice. Santa had to be inside at midnight or all was lost.

"I'll do it." It was The Red-Rider again. "I'll get you in."

"Dad, no!"

"Yes, son," he answered back, "your mother cannot lose

another child…Her last child. It would destroy her." In the distance Rendor could see her now, making her way from the back of the Elven troops towards them. He had to leave now. If she got there first he knew he might change his mind.

"But—"

"You tell her when you see her that I love her. I love you, too, son. Both of you more than I ever could have thought possible."

With that Santa climbed up on his friend's back and they flew. Straight up. Drawing the fire of the Halcyon troops as they did so. The others saw this and stormed the castle gates, the other reindeer taking to the sky again, trying to draw some of the fire their way. Klaaretteta saw it, too. She wondered which one it was. She wondered which loved one she would lose now. She tore into the Halcyon troops, screaming.

Donner watched, tears rolling down his face, as his father carried their leader towards the tops of the castle. He looked away before seeing his father cut down, knowing it would happen, not wanting that to be the last image of him he'd remember. No, he would forever remember the image of the two of them flying high up into the night sky, a glorious, blazing red comet.

He just prayed that his father did not die in vain. That in his ultimate moment he died a hero, his final mission a success. That he delivered Santa safely over the castle walls.

It was minutes from midnight. He guessed he would find out soon enough. They all would.

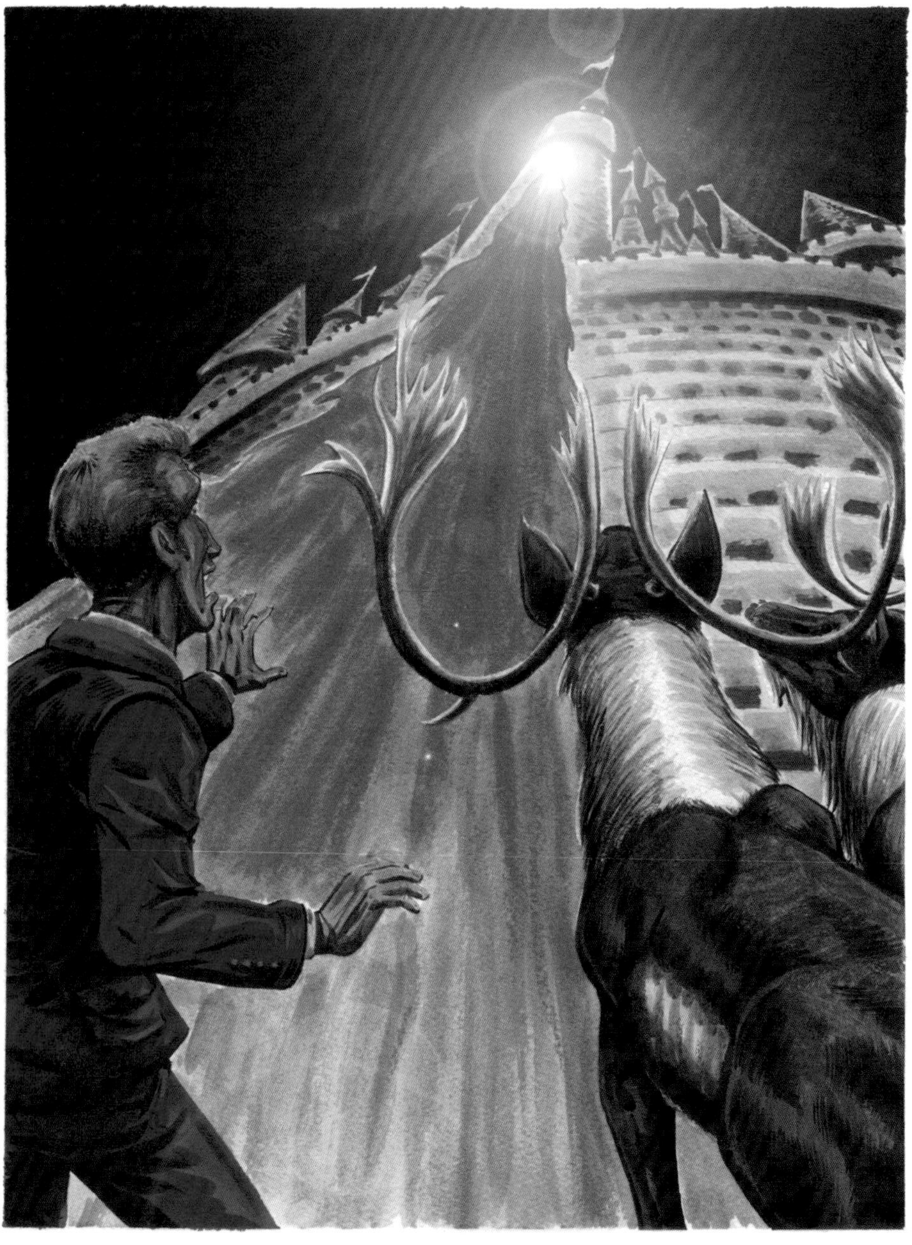

***

Urban legend is what most people thought it was. Other people would swear it was true. In some cases there was documentation verifying it, they would say. But where was the proof?

Urban legend.

Norbie would always laugh when a story would surface. Not out loud, of course, inwardly—to himself. Voices, radio transmissions, *God!* Just some of the things people claimed they heard coming from their dental fillings. It was funny, he thought, that after all these decades it never led back to him. He supposed it was because, A) the people making the claims were considered nutcases, and B) his technology was sophisticated and impossible to detect because it was augmented by Elven magicks.

But it was true. No urban legend. People *were* picking up transmissions…*Voices!*…Mostly Norbie's voice, in fact.

In the thirty-eight years since the Halcyon attack on the North Pole, and the disappearance of Santa Claus, Norbie was preparing. He was always very good at preparing—looking ahead. He figured that in those thirty-eight odd years he had treated somewhere between fifteen to twenty patients a day, approximately two hundred and fifty working days a year. Multiply that times the thirty, or so, years of practice and he figured he had probably filled somewhere in the neighborhood of two hundred thousand cavities. Quite a few. A few thousand of those were Halcyon employees as a matter-of-fact.

Couple that with the fact that about fifteen years ago he

patented the special filling material that he used and he himself invented—making himself, and Halcyon for that matter (as he was under contract with them at the time) a nice little fortune––allowing dentists around the world the use of this wonderful new dental material, he figured that there must be millions of people throughout the world with fillings he designed. Fillings he could transmit and receive signals through.

Fillings he could *talk* through.

For thirty-eight years Norbie whispered to them. Whispered to them while they slept.

He whispered the same short message time and time again…
"He lives…Santa Claus lives…As long as you believe in him! Never stop believing!"

***

Randall heard the voices again. This time he was sure of it—even in the thick of the battle he could hear them. Others heard them, too. The Halcyon soldiers were hearing them as well.

So was Sir Stephen.

It was fourteen minutes until midnight.

***

Santa landed hard! He couldn't be killed (actually he could as they would all soon find out) but he could be hurt, and he was pretty sure he just dislocated his left shoulder. His lower right leg also burned from where the rocket hit them. He looked up just in time to see The Red-Rider slam into the side of one of the castle towers. The impact was so tremendous that the sidewall of that tower virtually exploded from the force. The source of The Red-Rider's power was always a mystery—what was the source of that wonderful, glorious light?—no one knew for sure. But on this, his final day, it was more than evident that it was a very powerful force indeed. Granted, no doubt, by the gods. The explosion was tremendous.

When the dust settled Santa could see into the hole left behind. He saw them there… Norbie and the others! And Black Peter! He barreled through the troops now running at him, and to the doorway that would lead to the staircase that would take him to the top of that tower.

That would take him to Black Peter.

***

Norbie had seen Sir Stephen several times for dental examinations. With his advanced years it was completely plausible for this man to require extensive dental work—bridges, root canals, crowns and, of course, fillings…Lots of fillings. During these exams Norbie also had time to examine and explore the wonderful chair that Sir Stephen was confined to: a magnificent array of medical devices, gadgets and whatnot keeping him alive. *It must require a great deal of power to operate,* he thought. He was astonished when he saw the chair's powerful battery. *The chair was sophisticated, sure, but it didn't need* this *kind of power!* After a thorough investigation Norbie discovered that the chair was even more amazing than he initially thought. *My God!* thought Norbie, knowing then how they captured Santa all those years ago. Norbie took the liberty of making a few...*enhancements* to the chair. He found that he could add a few new devices of his own without losing any of the medical equipment's integrity. For instance, he was able to, quite easily, add a very sophisticated transmitter and receiver (his own design, of course). Not in the chair itself, though—no the chair was just for the power source—the transmitter and receiver were both in Sir Stephen's mouth. His mouth contained one of the most sophisticated transmission and receiving stations on the entire planet. What better place for it, Norbie always thought...The safest place in all of Halcyon... The one place they would've never thought to look. Norbie was quite proud of his work.

It was pure luck that Black Peter would be the one to provide the one last missing piece to complete Norbie's puzzle.

Norbie checked it all over one last time before flipping the switch—one of Sir Stephen's upper left incisors.

It was at that moment that The Red-Rider crashed into the tower and the wall to Norbie's right exploded inward!

***

Santa shattered the door with one mighty kick—a door that

was supposed to withstand the blast from a handheld grenade launcher. He entered a bloodbath—the bodies of fallen Elves lying everywhere, not always intact—and the sight of someone he hadn't seen in thirty-eight years about to tear Klondike Saskatchewan in half. And there behind them Norbie and a bloody Black Peter, a pick-axe sticking out from his chest, Black Peter's whip wrapped tightly around Norbie's throat.

"STOP!" was all that Santa said. And they did…at least for the moment.

He looked to the Abominable Snowman with a firm but gentle look and held out his hands motioning for him to put Klondike down. He did, his rage temporarily subsiding.

"Well, well, well!" sniped Black Peter, jerking on his whip causing Norbie more pain, choking the life out of him.

Santa proceeded with caution now. He knew that with one quick jerk Black Peter could decapitate Norbie. Black Peter knew it too and used Norbie now as a shield—a hostage. Santa had to play this just right if he were to save them.

Santa reached into his coat and removed it—a small piece of cardstock. It was a postcard! Black Peter could see that now. He recognized it! The last one they sent out a few months back. He recognized it because it was he who approved the final design. He could see it even from fifteen feet away, the illustration of a jolly Santa Claus waving from his sleigh, the beautiful reindeer pulling him through the star-filled sky.

"What is that?" Black Peter asked, laughing. "Have you done all of this to deliver me my mail?!"

"Yes," said Santa, "in fact, I have."

Santa walked closer to Black Peter now. As he approached the Halcyon soldiers were filing into the room through the door

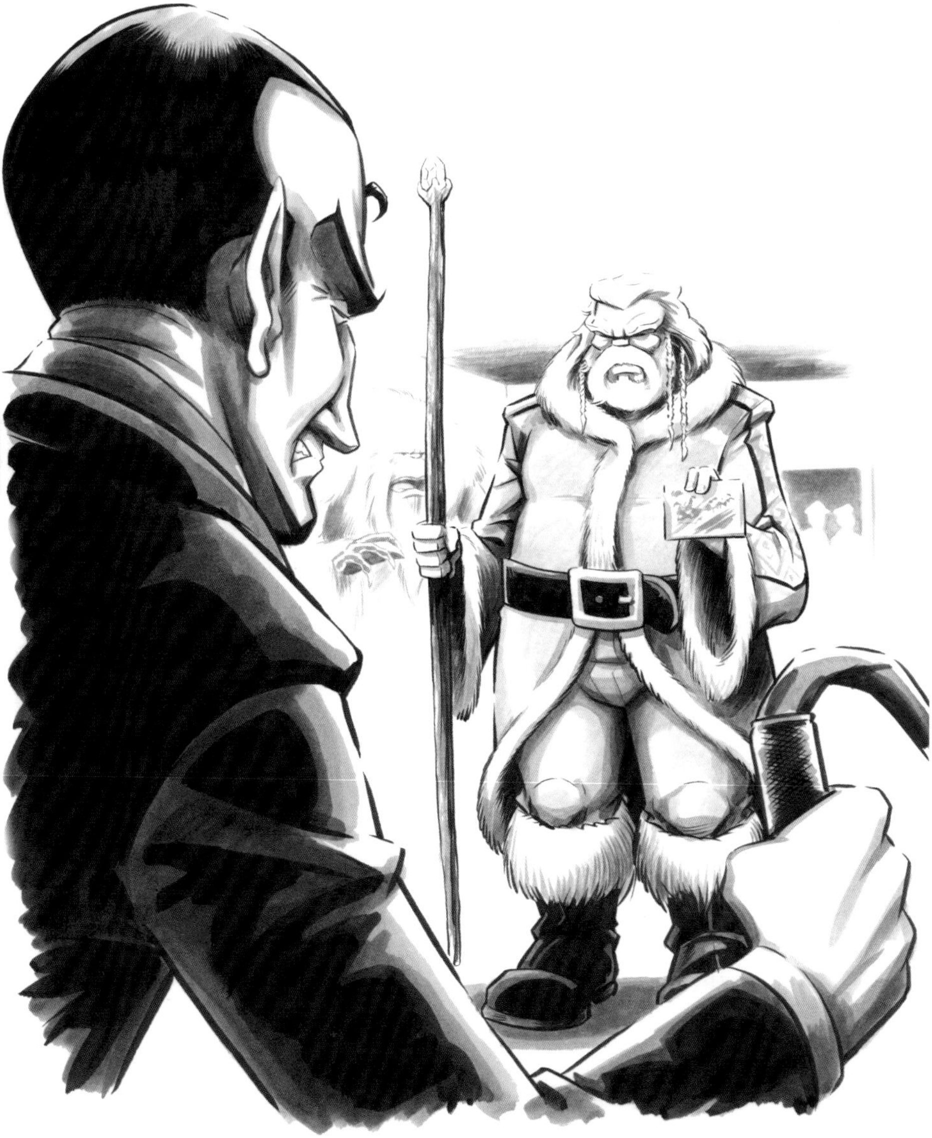

he just kicked down, led by their generals. From behind Santa Black Peter held up his hand to the generals, staying their hands. Santa continued…

"These were very clever, Peter. Very clever, indeed."

"Thank you. I thought so as well."

"Of course they would prove to be your undoing."

Black Peter said nothing now. No clever little quips or comebacks. Clearly puzzled.

"Oh yes," Santa explained, "had you not sent these…Had you not been so greedy, you really could have killed me."

Black Peter's eyes tightened. He responded, "You can't be killed…we tried."

"Yes, I remember. I was there. You're a fool Peter. Blinded by your hatred and greed. They kept me alive you idiot! And you helped them."

"What do you mean?" asked Black Peter, venom in his mouth.

"Don't you understand anything? Adults created me so many centuries ago as a way to get their children to behave, and the children did. Yes, adults created me, but it was the children that gave me *life!* Millions and millions of children believed in me. If enough people believe in a god—*really believe*—that god will exist! And the children believe *absolutely*…Their belief is pure! They *never* doubt!"

Black Peter's eyes widened now. He understood now where he failed. What a fool he was.

"Had you simply sent these cards of yours explaining that I was dead, and then explained how Halcyon would take over and uphold the '*tradition*' of Christmas your greedy ploy could have worked! There would have been doubt at first, of course…

The children would still believe me alive...until they saw the gifts that you had chosen. Then they would have believed you. They would have believed me dead. And I would have died. Without the children I am nothing.

"It was your hatred wasn't it? Having me dead wasn't enough."

Black Peter did not answer, just stared at Santa with barely contained rage.

"No, you wanted to destroy what Christmas was all about. You wanted to be relevant again, didn't you, Peter? Taking the good out of Christmas would be another victory for you, wouldn't it?"

There was a long pause before Black Peter finally did respond. One could almost feel the weight of his words.

"YES...I WOULD DESTROY CHRISTMAS! DESTROY EVERYTHING THAT YOU BELIEVED IN! CORRUPT THEM ALL! THEY'RE ALL GREEDY BY NATURE! AND THEN, ONE DAY, MAYBE DIG YOU UP AND SHOW YOU WHAT I HAD DONE! AND THEN BURY YOU AGAIN FOR ANOTHER HUNDRED YEARS!

"TELL ME...WHAT DID YOU THINK ABOUT WHILE YOU WERE DOWN THERE THE LAST THIRTY-EIGHT YEARS? DID IT HAUNT YOU EVERY SINGLE DAY WONDERING WHO HAD DONE THIS TO YOU?!" Peter laughed loudly now.

"Yes," Santa answered, "I had a lot of time to think while buried down there. A lot. But the thing that kept me going was the same thing that kept me alive...Hope. I had hope, Peter. I knew that as long as I remained alive down there that the children must still believe in me. I didn't know why, or how, but I knew that they still believed."

"Well," said Black Peter, smiling again, "I'm so glad we had this little talk. I feel much better now. I'll be sure now not to make the same mistake twice."

He tilted his head towards his generals now, his eyebrows arched. One of the generals responded.

"The gates are secure, sir. We have his army held in check."

"You see my dear old friend…your army faces defeat. They are outside the safety of the castle gates. Need I remind *you* of the castle's capabilities?"

He needn't. Santa was fully aware of them. Fully aware of the fail-safes it had against invaders…Fully aware that his entire army would be defeated given time. The castle was nigh invincible. He knew…he created it.

"No," Santa said at last, "you needn't. I am fully aware. But I'm curious," Santa continued, "don't you at least want to read your mail first?"

This surprised Black Peter. He had completely forgotten the postcard by now.

"Excuse me?"

"Your mail…your postcard." Santa stood there. Holding the card out in front of him. Not moving an inch.

Peter motioned for a soldier to get it, not wanting to get too close to Santa in case he tried something. The guard cautiously grabbed the card. Santa did nothing to stop him, just stood there calmly. The guard ran the card to Black Peter while keeping his eyes locked on Santa.

Black Peter read the card. He read it again. His face turned red.

"We intercepted them three months ago."

"McMahon!" spat Black Peter.

"Yes, Randall has proven to be quite helpful. Norbie was quite clever in recruiting your supervisor of shipping and receiving."

Black Peter shot Norbie a hateful glance. Nothing new there. Norbie gave him an almost apologetic shrug and smile.

"It was his idea to ask the kids to all do that, too." Santa pulled out his pocket watch now and looked at it. "By the way, they've all heard everything we've said since I've been in the room."

All the color ran out of Black Peter's face. His grip slackened on the whip...just enough.

The parents of the world were all a bit puzzled by the last postcard but they did as it asked. They didn't usually like letting their children stay up so late on Christmas Eve but this sounded important. The card read...

"Dear Parents of all the good little boys and girls around the world!

Greetings from the North Pole! Christmas time is almost here once again, and Santa needs your help this year! Santa is going to send all the good little boys and girls a secret message this Christmas Eve! And when the children hear it Santa will need them to sing for him...Louder than they've ever sung before. So listen for it kids! Just before midnight on Christmas Eve! And after you hear Santa's message he'd like you to sing his favorite song, 'Santa Claus Is Coming To Town!'

Thank you and Merry Christmas!"

The card still also contained the part of Halcyon's original message detailing costs and such as to not arouse any parents' suspicions. But the singing part was new.

Norbie felt the tension slacken a little and jerked away as hard as he could. He tore free from the whip but it would be quite some time before he would speak without pain again—the whip ripping away at his throat. Norbie lunged for Sir Stephen—for his mouth—he flipped another switch…a different tooth this time.

"SING FOR US, CHILDREN! *SING!*" shouted Santa.

Santa's words momentarily confused Black Peter. Until he heard the singing. It was coming from Sir Stephen…from his *mouth!* It came from others now as well. From their mouths! Not as loud as from Sir Stephen's but you could hear it nonetheless! Children singing! Singing *Santa Claus Is Coming To Town!*

"A wonderful…device…this chair…" Norbie croaked painfully, his good hand holding his throat, "…powered by your nuclear battery…your *'bomb'*…your *'Time Suppressor!'*"

Black Peter looked shocked. He pressed a button on a small hand-held device. He pressed it again…Nothing happened.

"It's a…clever device," Norbie continued, "…you used it to help keep him alive, didn't you?...all these years…the chair and a little elven magick…

"…was your failsafe, too…wasn't it?...In case it 'hit the fan' up here…you'd just activate…activate the chair at midnight…when Santa stopped Time. Up here…at the Pole… the convergence of the…uhhn…two timelines would be catastrophic!"

Black Peter snarled.

"Yes…wonderful device…" Norbie choked, struggling to

speak. "I'm using it… to power my transmitter…works like a charm!

"But still needed The List…to…to amplify…to boost my signal…the connection to the…the children…'Plan B.'" It was painful to do so, but Norbie finished with a smile, "Thank you."

The List. He put it there himself in Sir Stephen's lap! Damn the dentist! He should have killed him when he first saw him!

Halcyon's troops were baffled—all visibly shaken up—the generals as well.

Santa spoke to them. "These are the voices of the children, generals! Millions of them singing for me! Millions and millions of children that just heard the conversation between your leader and myself. They know now. They know. Are you going to kill all of them as well?"

The generals were horrified by the thought of it all and it showed by the expressions on their faces.

"YES!" Black Peter screamed. "WE WILL KILL EVERY SINGLE ONE OF THEM! IT DOESN'T MATTER! NONE OF IT MATTERS! WE STILL HAVE THE LIST! WE DON'T NEED CHRISTMAS ANYMORE, WE STILL HAVE THE LIST! IT WILL WORK WITH OR WITHOUT HIM, I'VE SHOWN YOU THAT! WE CAN STILL RULE!... TOGETHER!" He looked at the generals, "YOU CAN JOIN ME HERE AND RULE WITH ME! WE CAN STILL CONTROL THE OTHER COUNTRIES WITH THIS BOOK! BUT FIRST WE NEED TO RID OURSELVES OF HIM! ONCE AND FOR ALL!" He pointed at Santa. "WHATEVER THE COST!

The singing could still be heard.

"No!" it was Sir Stephen now who spoke. Spoke through the singing voices which were also coming from his mouth. "You shall not harm the children! I will not allow it!"

"SHUT UP OLD MAN!" shouted Black Peter, "*I* AM HALCYON NOW! I ALWAYS HAVE BEEN, FOOL!... YOU WERE MY PAWN! HAVE BEEN SINCE YOU WERE A LITTLE BOY, STEPHEN! DO YOU REMEMBER ME COMING INTO YOUR ROOM EACH CHRISTMAS? IT WAS ME WHO'S KEPT YOU ALIVE ALL THESE YEARS!... ME!!

"IT WAS ME WHO ORCHESTRATED YOUR DOWNFALL WITH THE 'BLACK FEATHERS,' YOU IDIOT! IT WAS ME WHO ORCHESTRATED HIS DOWNFALL!" he said pointing to Santa. "*I* AM HALCYON!"

He pointed to the soldiers. "THEY WILL FOLLOW ME!"

The generals looked at one another saying nothing. Finally one spoke.

"No, we will not slaughter children!"

Another echoed him and then another and another after that … But not all of them. Not all. It was as Santa feared. He would gather some to his side—the ones with some good still in their hearts—but not all. Greed was a powerful evil. You could see the generals and the soldiers begin to divide now. Soon they would be fighting amongst themselves. Soon the fighting would begin again. Black Peter would give the order to the soldiers at their stations to fire upon Santa's army outside. Some would and some wouldn't, but it didn't matter, enough of them would to kill more of his friends.

Black Peter sensed it, too, and laughed. "YOU SEE! I WILL YET STILL WIN THE DAY!" He began screaming orders again—to those in the room, over the intercoms to the soldiers at their stations and to the Abominable Snowman. "KILL THEM ALL!"

The poor beast reached out again towards Klondike and then…

MIƉNIGᴙT...

"No, you shall not kill anymore." And with that Santa began
to chant in the old language again. His ploy had bought him just
enough time. It was midnight now. It was midnight and he was
where he needed to be for this to work. He was inside the castle
and with The List. Directly on top of the North Pole where his
magicks were their strongest. Midnight: the only time it could
work; The castle on top of the North Pole: the only place it
could work; The List: its connection to the good children of the
world required to make it work; and Santa Claus: the magickal
being that bound them all together. All the elements required.

Time stopped.

Everything stopped. Well, not everything, just the human
world. Not the magickal one. This meant that Santa and all his
Elves still moved forward, including Norbie, including Black
Peter. It meant that all the magickal creatures of Santa's world
still moved forward with them. The Elves and the reindeer
were free to move safely now that the Halcyon troops and their

153

bullets stood frozen in mid-air before them.

Donner shot skyward now towards the tower his father crashed into. He lowered himself to the ground where his father tore through the tower wall. He stood over the spot where his father died. But just for a moment. And then he charged Black Peter.

"You've lost, Peter," Santa said. "You've lost."

Donner crashed into the back of Black Peter. So great was the impact that two of Donner's tines broke off, lodged deep in Black Peter's back. Black Peter was thrown forward to the ground, screaming in pain and outrage. But still he held onto his whip.

All Santa's magickal creatures could move forward with time stopped…All of them…including the Abominable Snowman.

He wasn't reaching *for* Klondike Saskatchewan as Santa stopped time, he was reaching *past* him—moving him aside so he could reach Black Peter…The little one with the whip! He no longer feared this evil little creature, no longer feared his whip. He picked him up as Black Peter screamed, remembering what Black Peter said to him but a few minutes ago, *'And this time rip the little bastard apart before swallowing him you big toothless idiot!'*

epilogue:

After all the dust settled Santa stood amongst his comrades–
–A-Bomb sitting off to the side cleaning his fingernails with
Klondike's axe (the Abominable Snowman wasn't the smartest
of Santa's creatures but he knew enough to remove the axe
from Black Peter's chest before eating him). Time was still at
a standstill. His Elves gathered the Halcyon troops that fought
against them, disarmed them, and then carefully moved their
suspended bodies to a secured location outside the castle; the
generals to a secured holding area within. They then proceeded
to carefully pluck as many of the flying projectiles from the air
and place them in an area where they would do no harm once
time began anew and they continued their deadly flight. The
top Elf scientists and weapons experts would disassemble the
nuclear "Time Suppressor" that was Sir Stephen's chair safely
now with Time standing still. They'd sort everything else out
later.

Santa was able to note a few that refused the final order given
by Black Peter, including Sir Stephen, and they would all be
treated accordingly at the trials. He was certain though that Sir

Stephen would likely not survive until the trials. He sensed that with Black Peter now gone Sir Stephen would fade quickly, the link between them—the power that Black Peter fed him—now cut.

Santa spoke quickly to his loyal comrades, "Quickly now! All is not lost this Holiest of nights! We can still save this Christmas." He looked to one of his Elf generals. "Are the hubs still in place?"

"Yes, all of them sir. And well-stocked with toys."

"I would be honored to lead you, sir." It was Donner.

"No, son, the honor would be mine." Santa placed his hand on Donner's neck. "You do your father's memory proud."

Donner wept.

"And the others? The other reindeer…"

"Most of us made it, sir. Most of us are still alive. Willing and able!" It was another reindeer limping in through the main gates of the castle. Behind him walked dozens more, some of them visibly wounded. Klaaretteta was with them now as well. She ran to Donner and they embraced, sharing their grief, the celebration for them bittersweet.

"Then we shall do our jobs!" Santa shouted in triumph, "Tonight we celebrate this most holy of nights! Tonight the good children shall receive the toys of Santa Claus and his noble family! Where is The List?!"

Norbie brought it to him now, safely disconnected from Sir Stephen. His wounded right hand crudely bandaged. Santa smiled at him sympathetically.

"I'm proud of you my boy…so very, very proud. You have the heart of a lion."

Norbie hugged Santa, his throat too swollen to speak now.

This was the first time they'd seen in each other in over three decades...The first time Santa had ever seen Norbie at a loss for words.

The moment was broken by IceCap entering the room. He carried a body. It was Randall.

"He-he died saving me…There was a flamethrower…One that we missed. It-it's not fair. He-he doesn't even know that he's won."

Santa and the others walked over to them, Santa carrying the mighty book…the powerful tome that so many had died for. The List. He stood next to IceCap and opened it. Right to the exact page, and showed him.

"He knows."

There on the page was Randall McMahon's name. And next to it was a single word.

"Good."

THE END

Acknowledgements

I would like to, first off, thank Stephen King and Berni Wrightson because it was their book, Cycle of The Werewolf, that so absolutely captured my 17 year-old imagination the Christmas of 1985, and had me firmly planted on the family couch for the three hours following the opening of this gift from my mother (special thanks to mom for buying me the book, too!). I was completely enthralled by Cycle Of The Werewolf!...Its striking cover, format, size, the wonderful illustrations and, of course, the fact that it was a book by Stephen King! I remember, vividly, my being so impressed by the book and thinking, "I want to do something like this someday!" Well, here's my "something like this!" 22 years later.
Maybe some 17-year-old kid will have the same reaction to this book this Christmas and we'll see their book 22 years from now.

Also special thanks must go out to the following people for their immeasurable help putting The List together…
Rob Venditti and Wayne Beamer for their editing help! Man, I can't believe how pitiful I am when it comes to proper punctuation.
C.J. Bettin for helping out with the cover design! C.J.'s a pal from way way back and is always there to help on my book projects. Thanks, Carly.
Max Estes for his help assembling the book in yet another one of those fancy-schmancy computer programs I know nothing about! Max is, perhaps, one of the most patient people I've ever met (must be the vegetarian diet!).
The fine folks over at Diamond Comics Distribution for their continued support with my publications. Especially Leah Deyneka and Steve Leaf!
The many fine retailers who have always supported me and my books, and the readers who buy them.
All the wonderful writers, artists and visionaries who have brought us so many wonderful tales of Christmas over the centuries. Their efforts have delighted children and helped make Christmas a magical part of our lives.

And finally my wife Sandy and my daughter Stella. Sandy has never wavered in her support of my chasing this dream of being a writer and Stella just thinks it's cool that daddy draws pictures with her.

About the Author...

Rich Koslowski started reading comic books when he was five years old. In the fourth grade he knew that being an artist was what he wanted to be when he "grew up." He hasn't quite "grown up" yet but at least his dream of being an artist (and a writer, too!) came true. He has written and illustrated for television, children's books, comic books and graphic novels professionally since 1990. He is best known for his creator-owned series The 3 Geeks and his graphic novels, Three Fingers and The King. His work has been nominated for the Eisner Award, Harvey Award, Ursa Major Award and has won the prestigious Ignatz Award in 2003 for his graphic novel, Three Fingers. In 2007 production on The 3 Geeks movie started. Rich is slowly—very slowly—conquering the world.

Visit Rich at RichKoslowski.com

A NOTE FROM THE AUTHOR...

The initial outline for this book was completed and I was in the early stages of illustrating a few of the pictures when, in researching other names for Santa Claus and the exact point of his origin, I stumbled upon Black Peter. I had never heard of the character...No, he was not a product of my warped imagination I just took him and "ran" with him in my own warped way. It seems that Black Peter was conjured up at, or around, the same time the myth of Santa himself was first conceived. He was created as a counterpart to Santa—Santa's "Ying," or would it be "Yang" in this case? Whatever...Black Peter is real—has been around since Santa—but for obvious reasons was fazed out of our Christmas lore many, many years ago. In telling people of my book over the past couple of years I have been surprised to learn that anyone at all has heard of Black Peter, but a few people actually have...Maybe he still visits them on Christmas Eve night?

Personally, I think he's a great character for the purposes of this book but other than that?...I think it's best he be forgotten.